"Journey of The Heart" Series

Vol. 1

"To Those Who Mourn"

Clem Stack Publications Ltd.

POEMS

Poems are groups, of words,
brought to life,
by thoughts,
pen,
and ink.
Like the dew
of a thought,
the ink produces,
its magic
of combined words,
that can make,
you,
perhaps millions,
think.

Clement Stack
28/11/2004

Clem Stack Publications Ltd.

15, Flower Hill,
Rushbrooke Manor,
Cobh,
Co. Cork,
Ireland.

Tel. No. 021- 4812051
Email: clemstack@eircom.net

A copy of this book can be obtained from:

Trinity College, Dublin
The Universities of Oxford and Cambridge
The National Library of Scotland
The National Library of Wales

These poems are dedicated to the "mourning heart"

INDEX

1

TO THOSE WHO MOURN

Try not to distract the traveller,
who is journeying to the light.
They are returning to the creator,
let them travel with all their might.
Rejoice at their newfound gain,
and not at your selfish loss,
regardless of the circumstances,
they have gone to meet the boss.

By weeping for your loved one,
you can make sad the soul,
distract them on their journey,
and interfere with their goal.
When they reach their new destination,
beyond the comprehension of man,
the sick are released from their illness,
and their burdens are placed in the can.
Their life's purpose has come to an end,
a purpose we can know little of,
if you truly have loved them, release them,
and wish them a good journey's end.

I release you now, my loved one,
from all your attachments to me,
I wish you a pleasant journey,
and now I set you free.
I will not interfere with your journey,
nor punish myself, at your loss,
I will treasure you in my memories,
and rejoice, at you, meeting "The Boss".

DANCE OF THE THOUSAND STARS

They danced the dance,
of the thousand stars,
as they realised,
they were not dead at all.

They danced the dance,
of the thousand stars,
for the soul,
must obey the call.

They danced the dance,
of the thousand stars,
on realising that death,
was the transport home.

They danced the dance,
of the thousand stars,
in the heavenly worlds,
to roam.

They danced the dance,
of the thousand stars,
when they realised,
they were not dead at all.

THE SEASONS OF CIRCLES

The rain, the rain, is falling,
on the graves, the rain is falling,
but there is nobody there,
because their souls, are out of their bodies.

That is not to say, do not remember,
no-one said you should not care,
remembering our dear loved ones,
is more than a memory, in the air.

And the snow, the snow, is falling,
on the graves, the snow is falling,
but there is nobody there,
because their souls, are out of their bodies.

As you look down on their marking place,
and the tears are in your eyes,
pay respect to your loved one,s body,
taking time to glance, at the heavenly skies.

And the wind, the wind, is blowing,
on the graves, the wind is blowing,
but there is nobody there,
because their souls, are out of their bodies.

Why not investigate the reincarnation,
it will open up your eyes,
the creator always grants the rebirth,
as we return from the heavenly skies.

And the sun, the sun, is shining,
on the graves, the sun is shining,
but there is nobody there,
because their souls, are out of their bodies.

We are much more, than our bodies,
not to be seen in our sleeping state,
wake up from your coma,
your investigation, is never too late.

And your light, your light is burning,
feel it all around your head,
it,s a greeting from your aura,
perhaps enough has been said.

FORGIVENESS IS NEVER TOO LATE

The heart of the matter, is why we were born to thee,
and in all this uncertainty, with whom did we agree?
Where is it written, and where is it to be found?
The recognition of this matter, is my thinking sound?
Many years of turmoil, did we have to embrace?
The end of this matter, is that we are no disgrace.
Now we are on our own, their time is coming to an end,
how many hours of contemplation, do we have to spend?
What were our lessons and did we learn them well?
Now that it is nearly over, can we break the spell?
Have they made us harder, or did they make us kind?
Questions to the heart, and to the heart I do remind.
Remember, to this you did agree, for they were only seeds,
the seeds to new futures, the seeds to a new need.
For now we know, how not to go, we learned the lessons well,
it's nearly their departing, it's time to break the spell.
But the storms of bad memories, that dwell in the mind,
to these departing souls, this is most unkind,
regardless of what happened, karma has to be paid
to help them on their guiding way, love cannot be delayed.
So thank them for the lessons, regardless of good or bad,
it's important to these departing souls, not to leave so sad.
This must be the greatest of lessons, how to let go,
for them, time has grown old, it's their time to go.
So while still in the living years, forgiveness is never too late,
or St. Peter, will have to do it for us,
when he greets them at the gate.

THE GRAVE SLAVE

It saddens me to see you,
spend so much time at the grave,
you have become the victim,
attachments, have made you the slave.

If I could only convince you,
that I am not there,
you would rid yourself of tension,
and end all the despair.

There is no one in that grave,
except my old space suit,
and please believe me dear,
it does not look so cute.

If you would listen to my whispers
and wake up to see your light,
all your sorrows would be over,
and you will see your cosmic light.

If you could only see from this side,
how things on earth are done,
with all the fast living,
we forget to have some fun.

I know that you are asleep,
asleep is your cosmic state,
attachments are glued to you,
of that I can relate.

Wake up and smell the roses,
that you have placed on my grave,
take some time for thinking,
for you have become the Grave Slave.

I am not there,
I rest now, in my old home,
I am happy in my new vibration,
these heavenly worlds to roam.

But it sure does disturb me,
in my new vibrational state,
when I see you at the graveside,
with all your sorrows to relate.

There is nobody in that grave,
it is just a box of bones,
your sorrow, is but an illusion,
your attachments are the stones.

Wake up and smell the roses,
that you have laid on my grave,
and the angels, will say to you,
stop being the "Grave Slave".

LET GO AND LET GOD

The body is in shock now,
after hearing the dreaded news,
what did you do to deserve this?
Sounded, one of your views.

But try to see it this way,
and maybe you will change your view,
it is time to desert your body,
and be one with the cosmic stew.

The longer you try to hold on,
the greater will be the pain,
for when this part is over,
comes the recognition, of no gain.

For one reason or another,
your body has commenced the shutdown,
your soul will be released from your body,
I hope you go out at your crown.

If this is the reality of the situation?
Or is it really just time to go home?
Guaranteed is the life ever after,
the cosmic heavens to roam.

It is time to do, the unfinished business,
so why not shower them all with love,
for you will just go out of your body,
as gracefully, as the flight, of a dove.

So why not throw a party,
to try to lighten their fears,
it should be a party to remember,
but not a party of tears.

So say goodbye to everyone,
you don't need permission to die,
you are finished with your body,
anything else is a lie.

Your body may have got too old,
or been inflicted with some disease,
the leaving of your body,
will bring your soul to ease.

You are your cosmic soul,
your soul is your conscious state,
for the second you get out of your body,
with the above, you can relate.

There is nothing you can do to stop it,
if you hold on, you just slow it down,
you review your life's video,
this memory, is in your chakra crown.

So release yourself from your body,
try to relax and just let go,
like steam coming out of the kettle,
a vibration of cosmic glow.

So drink your tears of laughter,
and swallow your attachment pill,
trust yourself to let go,
your body's vibrations, seek to be still.

Let go now, my cosmic friend,
come out, and see the light,
your new vibration is your transport system,
take flight to, the glorious light.

Learn fast, to trust yourself,
it is time, to leave earth's sod.
learn fast, to trust yourself,
by "letting go", and "letting God".

A PRAYER WITH THE DYING

There is no such thing, as death,
for death is no more,
than a rebirth,
into your true state.

It is a going home process,
and to complete the task,
you must leave your body behind.

Death as we know it,
is but an illusion,
as you will soon see, for yourself.

Call gently,
when you are ready,
for a departed loved one,
to help you with your transition,
and they will come,
to help and guide you.
This help is guaranteed,
you need only ask.

Your physical body,
will be left behind,
for it is not the true you,
this you will demonstrate,
to yourself shortly.
You do not need it anymore,
for it is time to go home,
to take your rest.

When you are ready,
and in your own time,
let go gently,
and embrace the mystery.

This so called mystery,
is no mystery for,
as you were born into a physical body,
you had to experience,
a form of death to do it,
and now it is the reverse situation,
only your body will perish,
you will not,
please trust me on this one,
I have no reason to lie to you,
only your body will die.

I will stay with you,
I will encourage you,
I will help you, in every way,
but I will not force your mind.
All I offer is encouragement, my cosmic friend,
to make this flight,
the flight out of your body
You will not be dead
only your body will die.

The energy in your body,
will leave with you,
it is a great part of you,
your body will become lifeless,
for you will not be in there anymore.
You will experience this fact, as
you view your body,
nobody is dead,
nobody dies,
death is just, coming out of your body.

So as I hold your hand,
and in your own time,
I invite you,
To let go,
And let God.

PLEASE, NOT SO HARD

I am standing here beside you,
but me you cannot see,
please do not mourn me,
with you I do plea.

My lifetime here is over,
a new one has just begun,
I will greet you, in this new world,
when your time on earth, is done.

I am only out of body,
it seems so hard to understand,
my cosmic state and journey,
brings me, to the homeland.

So now you must release me,
and let my spirit be free,
I react to your vibrations,
when you mourn too hard for me.

All these earthly attachments,
they are a form of spell,
for when you mourn too hard for me,
my life becomes, a living hell.

I have met up with my spirit group,
all the details they did relate,
I will greet you, when your time is over,
I will meet you at the gate.

I thank you for this understanding,
it is so important to me,
I wish not, to be earth bound,
I wish only to be free.

I am cured now, of all the sorrow,
I am completely illness free,
cured entirely of all my ills,
no more doctors, no more pills.

Mourn not too hard, my loved ones,
especially, not too hard for me,
my earth's journey is over,
in these heavens I am free.

So as you stare at my body,
there is nobody at home,
I have come out and left it,
in my new vibration to roam.

As you are disposing of my body,
as you take it to its resting place,
I will review the ceremony with you,
but me, you cannot trace.

So when the ceremony is over,
I will begin my journey to the light,
please do not mourn too hard for me,
and cause turbulence on my flight.

So I say goodbye to one and all,
thank you for the time, shared with me,
drop all the attachments, please,
and let me be free.

GOD'S TELEPHONE NUMBER

The candle burned so brightly,
reflecting the face of the loved one who passed away.
For they promised, they would be here forever,
but God had the final say.
All that is left is the photograph,
of the loved one held so dear,
expensive now are the attachments,
identifying the understanding,
will someday, dispel the fear.

I want to talk to my loved one,
they cried out to their God.
I know it's only their body,
that lies here under the sod.
I want to talk to my loved one,
so put them on the land line.
Just give me the heavenly number,
I will dial with fingers divine.

I want to talk to my loved one,
that recently passed away,
we were not prepared for their departing,
now we have so much to say.
So please, call my loved one,
bring them on the line.
I desperately need to talk to them,
and hear them say everything is fine.

My understanding is always with you,
your understanding is not always the same,
for I am the creator,
and to me all creations must return.
Their journey, it is over,
regardless of what the calendar has to say,
they return on the appointed time,
their life's videos to display.

But can I talk to my loved one,
who recently passed away,
I am fed up with my frustration,
I have so much to say.
The healer gave me your number,
he said you were just a thought away,
if I could just calm down the frequency of my emotions,
would they hear all I have to say?

The advice he gave you is splendid,
someone has worked it all out,
talk in your silent mind,
but please do not shout.
Pray in a talking manner,
this frequency is static free,
for all my children return to me,
when it's your turn, it will be clearer to see.

Start by calming your emotions,
sometimes it can generate a cry,
for the returning of your loved ones,
is understanding why they had to die.
So go ahead and talk to your loved one,
for they are just a thought away,
talk gently to your loved one,
for they are listening to all,
you have to say.

TO THE "LORD GOD" OF OUR UNIVERSE - A

To the "Lord God" of our Universe,
please announce to those who have travelled before us,
that the last bell has been rung for our Loved One,
(Name) _____
Their life,s cycle has come to a close,
and the preparation for their journey has begun.
We evoke the powers of our ancestors,
to come swiftly to lend assistance,
in their ascension.

We request this transition period,
to be swift like the swallows,
to be as beautiful as your sunset,
to be guided into your true light,
in the heavenly dimensions.
For you have declared unto us,
that in your house,
there are many mansions.

We request, that the fire be lit,
the candles burning,
fruit and flowers be placed on the table,
and celestial music, to be played softly.
We request, that our brothers and sisters,
who have journeyed before us are given notice,
as to the arrival time, of our Loved One.

We evoke the energies of the light,
for those of us who must stay behind,
to complete our cycles and to let not,
the energy of sorrow, rise too high.

To the "Lord God" of our Universe,
let the mourning period, be of the flowers of annual.
We send cosmic praises and thanks,
as you gently remind us,
that we are not earth people,
enjoying a spiritual experience,
but spiritual beings,
experiencing,
a human experience.

To the Lord God of our Universe,
notice is hereby given,
(Name) _____ is preparing to go home.

TO "THE LORD GOD" OF OUR UNIVERSE - B

To the "Lord God" of our Universe,
please announce to those who have travelled before us,
that the last bell has been rung for our Loved One,
(Name) _____
Their life,s cycle has come to a close,
and the preparation for their journey has begun.

We evoke the powers of our ancestors,
to come swiftly to lend assistance,
in their ascension.

We request this transition period,
to be swift like the swallows,
to be as beautiful as your sunset,
to be guided into your true light,
in the heavenly dimensions.
For you have declared unto us,
that in your house,
there are many mansions.

We request, that the fire be lit,
the candles burning,
fruit and flowers be placed on the table,
and celestial music, to be played softly.
We request, that our brothers and sisters,
who have journeyed before us are given notice,
as to the arrival time of our Loved One.

We evoke the energies of the light,
for those of us who must stay behind,
to complete our cycles and to let not,
the energy of sorrow, rise too high.

To the "Lord God" of our Universe,
let the mourning period be of the flowers of annual.
We send cosmic praises and thanks,
as you gently remind us,
that we are not earth people,
enjoying a spiritual experience,
but spiritual beings,
experiencing,
a human experience.

To the Lord God of our Universe,
notice is hereby given,
(Name) _____ is on their way home.

HEART OF THE MATTER

The heart of the matter,
is a matter of the heart,
I was not expecting this,
it's tearing me apart.
Death comes so suddenly,
unexpected, at its best,
and the heart of the matter,
is a matter of the heart.

What can I say to you?
As you lie there so still,
this was not expected,
it's such a bitter pill.
Soul searching now, is the game,
things will never be the same,
and the heart of the matter,
is a matter of the heart.

Your last breath you have taken,
your body you have forsaken,
where are you now?
And what do you have to say?
You are not far from here,
it is just another, atmosphere,
and the heart of the matter,
is a matter of the heart.

I will live in our memories
be they good or bad,
for the time spent with you,
I am eternally glad.
And come the day without delay,
I will rejoice with you again,
And the heart of the matter,
is a matter of the heart.

I will honour all your wishes,
of this day, we did talk,
the emotions are running high now,
as behind you, I do walk.
My water gates are flooding,
things will never be the same,
and the heart of the matter
is a matter of the heart.

It's sad this day, as it comes to an end,
I wonder is it, the end, or a bend?
I am not sure what to think,
or what I should say,
I wish you a good journey,s end,
and all my love, I do send,
and the heart of the matter
is a matter of the heart.

ATTACHMENT FREE

These marking stones of various sizes,
death came late, a few surprises,
hard lessons learned on this trip,
are you the captain of your ship?

To unify the great three,
something of a mystery,
who teaches us, this stuff,
who is strong, to call the bluff?

Teachers wise called the sages,
shouted down, through the ages,
plenty of no notice, was the reply,
and we don't know what to do, when we die.

So why should death be a great mystery?
This great unification, of the three,
the father, son and the holy ghost,
don't stand to attention at the last post.

The mind, body, and the soul,
that's the secret, that's the goal,
in unifying all these three,
brings the end, to the mystery.

The soul is housed in its burden of flesh,
surrendered by the mind, grossly enmeshed,
and if there are attachments, to this earth,
it can only generate, a new birth.

No attachments of any kind,
that's the secret, free the mind,
easily said, but it can be done,
peace everlasting, coupled with fun.

So how do we stop this cycle of birth?
find the answer, free from this earth,
the answer is there for every soul to see,
of course the answer is "attachment free".

NOT THAT EASY

Do you sit there in your silence,
flavoured by your fears?
Wishing that someone,
could turn back the years.

The last bell has been sounded,
the call heard by one and all,
the respecting of the last wishes,
not that easy is your call.

The tears of flooding memories,
the task of letting go,
in the arena of attachments,
not that easy,
letting go,
and letting God.

The Spiritual Fields

Clem Stack

"Follow the trail series"

This impressive book sparkles with wit, insight and uplift and one cannot fail to be enriched by this author's positive and engaging approach to life. There is a judicious balancing of practice and precept in the structuring of the text, and lively scenarios are offered as affirmations of the concepts which the author has chosen to expound.

The text is totally free from any of the tiresome pretensions one has come to associate with literature of this sort, and Clem Stack has made it his business to demystify the workings of the mind and spirit and to demonstrate that untold degrees of enlightenment, i.e. the raising of our spiritual consciousness, are within our reach if we take the time to formulate a positive way of thinking. The author's great good humour shines forth from the text to the extent that we never feel as though he is condescending or preaching from a great and superior height.

This is a friendly book, and its author has much to share. The engaging style and thoughtful presentation will ensure that this book will be of appeal to a broad cross section of readers.

Future book titles:

The Spiritual Letters
The Spiritual Warrior

Journey of the Heart Series

GEOFFREY R. SHARPE is a Fellow of the I y .... of Chartered Surveyors, a Fellow of the Chartered Institute of Building and a member of the CIOB Building Conservation Forum. He is also a member of a Diocesan Advisory Committee for the Care of Churches and a past chairman of a building conservation trust. He is author of *Historic English Churches: A Guide to their Construction, Design and Features.*

Geoffrey R. Sharpe

Traditional Buildings of the English Countryside

An Illustrated Guide

I.B. TAURIS

LONDON · NEW YORK

Published in 2011 by I.B.Tauris & Co Ltd
6 Salem Road, London W2 4BU
175 Fifth Avenue, New York NY 10010
www.ibtauris.com

Distributed in the United States and Canada Exclusively by Palgrave Macmillan,
175 Fifth Avenue, New York NY 10010

ISBN: 978 1 84885 614 1 (hb)
         978 1 84511 841 9 (pb)

A full CIP record for this book is available from the British Library
A full CIP record is available from the Library of Congress

Library of Congress Catalog Card Number: available

Typeset by JCS Publishing Services Ltd, www.jcs-publishing.co.uk
Printed and bound in Great Britain by TJ International Ltd, Padstow, Cornwall

Contents

Illustrations

Introduction

The aim of this book is to provide those travelling around the English countryside with a better understanding of the variations in buildings in the different regions and the reasons why they occur. It is also an exposition on the diversity of old buildings in rural areas and the way people lived and worked in them. The range and complexity of the subject has imposed constraints on coverage, and with this in mind the text has been directed towards a clear and precise interpretation on the more fundamental aspects of rural building and living in earlier times. The appendices at the back list a wide selection of places to visit that have been chosen as being of particular appeal to anyone interested in the past.

1 The Landscape and How it Developed

Whilst much of the rural scenery in Britain is the outcome of evolution and the natural world, considerable changes have also occurred through human intervention. In reality some landscapes derive from the work of earlier generations whose activities have materially altered the appearance of the landscape.

The Early Forests

Much of England was at one time covered with dense forest, though by 1600 the wooded areas had been denuded to a point where good timber was becoming scarce. Up to that stage, timber had been used extravagantly for a variety of purposes, which included shipbuilding, pottery, iron and charcoal-making without proper regard to conserving resources. Afforestation started when the last Ice Age receded; and as the land became warmer and fertile, trees started to grow, the more successful species being birch, poplar, rowan, willow and fir. Later, a period of rising temperatures encouraged species such as oak, elm and hazel to take a firm hold. Oak in particular became prolific and can still be seen in large numbers in the south of England.

The Roman Legacy

The parts of Britain occupied by the Romans underwent changes that had a lasting impact on the natural landscape. A large number of historic towns in England have Roman origins, and many roads continue to follow the routes originally selected by Roman engineers. Before this, road communications had been by means of tracks running mostly along higher ground to overcome the problem of flooding in the winter months. The Romans, with improved knowledge and engineering skills, were able to build highways in lowland areas, and this had the effect of opening up new direct routes and created opportunities for increased trade, especially at the ports.

The Arrival of the Saxons and Vikings

The Saxon and Viking invasions between AD 400 and 1066 are also significant for they started the coming together of communities to form the village way of life familiar in the present day. The traditional village green, now the scene of cricket matches and local events, had defensive origins and was the place where cattle could be driven for protection against wolves and rustlers.

The Norman Conquest

The Norman Conquest in AD 1066 marked the start of an important phase in British history, with fundamental changes being made to the rule of law and the cultural development of the people. The Normans not only dispossessed the Saxon overlords of their lands but also built a range of fortifications to consolidate territorial gains made against a fickle and unreliable populace. Castles appeared in strategic places in the countryside and in existing towns, with the intention of subjugating inhabitants through an atmosphere of awe and fear. It is important to differentiate between a castle and a fort. Whilst fortifications may predominate over domestic features, a castle is in essence a protected residence, whereas a fort has purely a military purpose.

As the new rule became consolidated, the Normans found additional uses for their castles and used them as strongholds for the treasury. The castles also made convenient prisons and centres of administration, and were ideal for holding courts, meetings and hearings. The face of the countryside started to alter as well, with many marshland areas being drained and reclaimed, with neglected woodlands that had been denuded and allowed to grow wild being cleared and used for cultivation. The period between 1150 and 1500 was also a time of extensive building in both the towns and the countryside.

The Reform of Agriculture

Between 1750 and 1845, some areas in England underwent fundamental changes following the passing of the Enclosure Acts. Up to this time the pattern of farming in many parts varied little from medieval practices, and land was worked under a system of open fields divided into strips. The effect of this new legislation was to break up and remodel the landscape into a network of fields surrounded by hedgerows. The new field boundaries were mainly defined either by timber fencing or hedging – mostly of whitethorn or hawthorn. In areas where stone was freely available, fields were mostly enclosed with dry-stone walling. This is a technique whereby stones of various sizes are put together in a way that enables them to be assembled without the use of mortar. This change also saw the cutting of a system of shallow ditches for improved field drainage, which enhanced the fertility of the land.

The Industrial Revolution

After the Industrial Revolution the growing pace of change altered large areas of the countryside in both function and appearance, and networks of roads, canals and railways encroached into hitherto unspoilt farmland. The worst effects were to be felt from mining, which scarred and polluted the surrounding landscape. Today, many manmade features in the form of viaducts, aqueducts, cuttings, bridges, locks and roadways blend into the landscape and have become part of history.

2 *The Origins of Place Names*

English Place Names and How They Can Relate to Buildings and People

The Latin Origins

A host of curious and strange-sounding place names can be found around the regions of England, many of them having very early origins. Some are derived from the influence of either the Saxon or Norman occupations whilst others have been Anglicized from Latin and may even be a direct throwback to Roman times. Examples are *Londinium*, the Roman name for London, and *portus* (a harbour), from which comes Portsmouth. Local dialects and customs have also produced some odd names – sometimes for rather peculiar or unpredictable reasons. Moreover, the spoken English of today differs considerably from many of the terms, meanings and pronunciations used in the past. Some of the more perplexing names are frequently found to be hybrid and come from elements of two or more languages.

Saxon and Celtic Links

Names that stem from the Saxons can often be traced back to a local leader or dignitary. Hastings is believed to relate to *Haesta*, the name of the man who controlled a settlement in that area. Where *stead* features in a place name, historians believe that it is linked to a Saxon farmstead and has resulted in names such as Ashamstead or Oakhamstead, which are likely to have been associated with a farm located near a notable tree. If a name terminates in *ley* the meaning refers to a forest clearing or meadow, and well-known towns such as Camberley and Henley can be identified with this interpretation. Those places which end in *bury* have connections with a fortification or stronghold, and many are now large urbanizations or cities such as Shrewsbury, Newbury, Sudbury, Norbury, Salisbury and Bloomsbury. The Saxon influence also perpetuates in the much-used term 'borough', which comes from *beorg*, meaning a mound. Many towns – including Farnborough, Middlesbrough, Peterborough and Scarborough – have a relationship with this term. In the north of England the Celtic influence is clearly detectable. *Kirk* is Gaelic and has connections with Christianity, more notably an established church. This explains names such as Kirkbride and those with a similar connotation. Any name beginning with *bal* has Celtic origins, with *bally* being the Gaelic for village. Baldersly in North Yorkshire is one such example. *Ouse* is Celtic for water, which gives rise to names such as Ousefleet and Ouseburn.

The Norse Connections

The Norsemen who invaded England in the ninth century also left a legacy in place names, especially those that end with the attachment *by* which refers to a township or settlement. Names such as Selby, Derby, Kirby and Crosby all come within this category. In particular *kirby* refers to a village with a church and *crosby* a village with a cross. *Thorp* means settlement, which explains names such as Bishopthorpe, Althorpe and others. A further indication of an old Norse settlement is the term *thwaite*, which denotes a clearing in a forest or woodland or even thick overgrowth. Towns linked to this include Hawthornthwaite and Brackenthwaite. *Mor* refers to barren upland. *Tun* is more associated with a person; for example, someone with the name of Beorhthelm may well have been the origin of the place name Brighton.

The French Influence

The French influence arising from the Norman invasion was more in the use of particular words and expressions rather than in word terminations or adjuncts. Town names such as Theydon Bois in Essex, Ashby-de-la-Zouch and Belvoir in Leicestershire are examples of an obvious French connection. Some Old French names have, however, become Anglicized – such as Sandygate, which started as Sangatte. *Beau* means attractive, hence the name Beaulieu; *mal* refers to a difficult terrain or access. Herstmonceux in Sussex was the seat of the Monceaux family who were Norman.

The Legacy of Old English
Many of the Old English terms are self-explanatory, such as Swinford, which describes a ford – a place in a river or stream where it is shallow enough to be crossed by foot or vehicle – where swine were kept. *Stan* means stone, and Stanford refers to a place where a stone wall meets a ford. Sometimes place names are linked either to a religious establishment, such as a monastery, or to a lord of the manor. Names like Monks Risborough and Weston Favell are good examples. *Tring* is Old English for a tree-covered slope, and *weald* means a woodland. *Chart* is an old description for rough ground, and places such as Chartwell and Chart Sutton relate to this. *Stoke* is an old term for 'place' and Stoke Abbot for example, describes a place where land was once held by the Abbot of Sherborne. In the past, partitions known as *penns* were sometimes built within the waters of a river so that fish could be kept captive and alive until ready for consumption, so the name *penn* attached to any historical place name may have a direct connection with this practice, although the term was also used for an animal enclosure. *Den* is Old English for animal pastureland, giving substance to names like Crittenden and Hughenden. In the present day some names may not stand the test of logic or reason, but there are likely to be hidden answers.

Dereliction
Many early settlements, villages or hamlets (small villages) were destroyed by either invasion, conflict or economic decline, even though the place name may have survived. The plague known as the Black Death decimated many communities to the point of non-existence, and in some cases wealthy landowners relocated settlements to improve the amenities around a grand home, which sometimes entailed remodelling the local landscape. There are many areas around England where the remains of deserted villages can be found; most have a story to tell. Some place names have also fallen victim to the use of slipshod language and they cannot now be readily identified with the original spelling and interpretation.

~

Other Names with Interesting Origins

Ac   relates to oak, which has resulted in names such as Acton and Ackworth.

Addle   is Old English for a dung heap or latrine pit. This links with the place names such as Addlestone or Eddelston.

Ald   is early English for old, hence names such as Aldwick and Aldborough.

Ax and *ec*   link a place with water, hence Axminster and Exeter.

Bec   refers to a brook and has resulted in names such as Beckenham, Beckley and Beckhampton.

Castra   is an ancient term for a camp – hence names such as Lancaster.

Col   refers to a colony, Lincoln being a good example.

Combe   means a hollow and relates to places names such as Ilfracombe and Boscombe.

Dal   is an early term for a dale, hence names such as Arundel.

Ham   refers to a manor estate and has produced names like Hambrook and Holkham. Hamstead describes a farmstead that had been attached to a manor estate.

Hurst   means a wood: Lyndhurst and Midhurst.

Strata   means a street, hence Stratford and Stratton.

Wick   describes a town, which fits with Warwick.

Wich   is the old name for a creek, which gives meaning to place names such as Harwich, Ipswich and Greenwich.

~

1. Aisled barn

3 *Farm Buildings and Farming*

Old farm buildings can reveal much about an area and the method and type of farming undertaken, either now or in the past. The nucleus of any farm is the farmhouse around which a group of buildings have been formed to create a farmstead. They are usually close to a village, town or hamlet, but some are found well away from communities, often as the result of an original settlement having been relocated or deserted, leaving the farmstead in isolation. Buildings will not always be found in group form, and some may be located in other parts of a holding for a particular convenience or reason, such as the need to avoid a difficult terrain for carting or unnecessary journeying in the care of cattle. The essence of efficiency in a farmyard is compactness and an arrangement that is energy saving.

Farmstead Layouts
As a result, four standard layouts evolved that were found to meet these requirements, namely: the L shape, the U form, the E form and the enclosed square or compound. The size and number of buildings were influenced by the amount of land attached to the farm and the type of farming being practised. Adaptations of the basic design occur where there is a need to take advantage of a sloping site to drain effluent away from a cowshed or stable, and in locations that enable gains to be made from natural features or the prevailing wind. Also, there are some notable regional differences, such as the bastle houses, the longhouses and the laithe houses, which will be described later.

The Effect of Mechanization

As farming became more mechanized, all available forms of motive power were harnessed for threshing. Use of the flail was overtaken by either wind, water or horse power, and in some cases the steam engine – prompting a different form of barn design. Buildings that used machinery powered by horses (known as a horse engine) can be easily spotted by an addition which has a distinctive rounded or polygonal end (Fig. 2), with any other forms of machinery being housed in a plain rectangular structure set at right angles to the barn.

～ BARNS ～

THE THRESHING BARN

Until comparatively recent times barns were used jointly for the threshing of wheat, barley, oats or rye and for the storage of hay and threshed straw. Most can be readily identified externally by their shape and proportions, and the majority have been designed to a more or less standard layout, but regional variations are apparent. The basic design is rectangular with a centrally located threshing floor and two equally proportioned bays either side. Many of the larger barns are aisled and have sweeping roofs going down to low-level eaves (Fig. 1). The large tall entrance doors in the middle are a clear distinguishing feature, opening on to the threshing area, with double or single doors at the opposite side. Not only did this enable deliveries to be made at the source of the threshing operation but it also provided a draught and good light for winnowing the husks from the grain. In some districts the main doors will be found set in projecting porches that gave the threshing process added protection during spells of bad weather.

To prevent grain from being blown away and to stop animals from straying into the area of operation, loose boards that slotted into grooves were sometimes used as a temporary barrier during work. In order to minimize damage to a crop from damp and mould, extra ventilation was introduced by way of air vents around the walls. An original barn will have an abundance of these holes, worked to a pattern of small square or triangular openings or narrow vertical slits. In some parts of the country, barns built at first-floor level were favoured, in an effort to reduce the risk of infestations from vermin, with the ground floor being utilized for some other purpose.

2. Horse engine

The Tithe Barn

Many of the remaining old barns were originally tithe barns. A tithe was a tax levied on one-tenth of the annual produce from the land, imposed to support the parish priest and to enable him to maintain the fabric of church property and to provide relief for the poor. Produce raised for this purpose was stored in a nearby barn, usually being of modest proportions, but those serving the monasteries were often massive. In 1891 an Act of Parliament restricted the payment of tithes and the 1925 Tithe Act transferred tithe rent charges to Queen Anne's Bounty Fund, which had been established in 1704 for the benefit of the poorer clergy. Tithes were eventually extinguished by the 1936 Tithe Act.

The Granary

A granary is a building used for the storage of grain after it has been threshed and winnowed. A typical granary is a free-standing square or rectangular timber structure resting on a series of small piers. Granaries are mostly weatherboarded externally, but slate and tile cladding and brick nogging were also used. In order to help keep out rats and mice the flooring was always covered with tongue-and-groove boarding, and occasionally this

3. Granary on staddles

4. Cartshed with granary over

included the internal walls. It was, however, a more common practice to lath and plaster the walls internally. Mushroom-shaped piers known as staddles helped to reduce the likelihood of vermin climbing in from the ground (Fig. 3) – a feature more frequently found in the southern parts of England.

High-Level Storage
An alternative method of storage provided space above a cartshed, with access from outside steps together with a trap-door in the floor for loading directly into cartage underneath (Fig. 4). This is a feature more likely to be found in the midlands and north of England. Grain storage was also provided over stabling but, because of the risk of contamination, it was not considered a suitable location for grain held for human consumption. Some granaries form part of a building known as a mixing house (see below).

THE MIXING BARN

A mixing barn is normally a two-storey building located near the farmstead, in which animal feed can be ground and mixed, with a loft and loading door at first-floor level and a trap-door set in the floor. In the past, the mixing machinery was often operated by either a horse engine or steam power, in which case they can more usually be identified externally by the provision of an apse-shaped extension or a small projection with a chimney.

THE SHELTER SHED

Since the mid-nineteenth century, greater consideration has been given to the welfare of farm cattle, including the need to provide shelter during periods of severe weather. Prior to this it was more common to leave cattle in the open throughout the winter period. This switch in thinking led to the creation of the frequently seen enclosed yard with buildings attached. The open shelters now regularly seen around the countryside are not always confined to the farmyard and may be positioned in varying parts of the same holding (Fig. 5).

5. Small shelter shed

THE LINNY

A variation of the shelter shed is the linny or linhay, which mainly appears
in the south-western part of the country. This has an open shelter at ground
level, with open-fronted loft space overhead (Fig. 6).

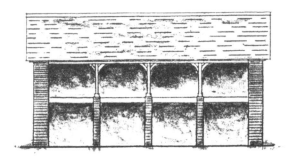

6. Linny

The Hay or Dutch Barn

Hay can quickly deteriorate when exposed to damp and needs to be kept covered and to have adequate cross-ventilation. Hay barns can take a number of different forms, but they always comply with this basic requirement (Fig. 7). Many of the surviving examples were built from the late 1880s onwards as a result of improved methods of production that enabled many farmers to grow a surplus that could be sold on.

7. Hay barn

8. Field barn

THE FIELD BARN

Field barns are sited away from the main farmstead to provide food, storage and shelter for animals in those parts of the holding that could only be reached with difficulty, particularly in an emergency or hostile weather conditions. For this reason they are generally smaller than those seen in the main farmstead but are similar in design and style. They first appeared in the seventeenth century, but as mechanization improved, together with better forms of transport, they have gradually became obsolete (Fig. 8).

THE COW HOUSE

Until more recent times cattle played a vital role in the economic and seasonal cycle of farming: they not only produced milk and cream but were also the source of local butter and cheese. Before the age of mechanization, oxen had been considered the ideal animal for haulage and ploughing, with store cattle giving an ample supply of meat. Moreover, they could be easily bred as an additional way of enhancing the annual income. A cow house was needed for control, care and breeding, and in most parts of the country they conform to a fundamentally similar layout (Fig. 9). They can usually be identified by the rectangular shape, the positioning of the doors and the equally proportioned windows along the entire length.

THE FARM STABLE

By the latter part of the eighteenth century the draught horse had supplanted the ox for use in carting and ploughing, a situation that remained largely unchanged until the tractor completely replaced the use of horse power towards the end the Second World War. As with cow houses, designs for stables follow a familiar layout in which the horses can be either tethered or kept in a loose box that allows them freedom of movement. Externally, the heck door (half door) at the entrance clearly identifies a farm stable (Fig. 10). Heck doors, although now regarded as a feature of stable design, are thought to have originated to give greater control of traffic at gatehouses. In some parts of England, especially in the south-east, it has long been a tradition for stable windows to be in the form of lunettes (half-circle shape).

9. Cow house

10. Stable

The Hemmel

An important variation of the loose box is the hemmel, which is larger and provides a walled external area that is about the same size as the internal space. An animal may have more freedom of movement in a hemmel, but the nature of the containment severely restricts normal exercise. In addition to being used by horses the hemmel is regularly reserved for fattening bulls and calves or when a cow is calving and needs special attention. If built to dimensions larger than normal it is more often termed a bull pen.

The Bank Barn

The bank barn enabled full use to be made of a sloping site (Fig. 11). It dates from the early eighteenth century and, whilst it is more usually seen in the Lake District, it is also found in other regions of Britain.

11. Bank barn

The Ash House

A small structure occasionally found near an original farmhouse is the ash house, which was used for the storage of ash from the open fire until needed for scattering over land as a nutrient. Made from stone, some are circular in shape and have either a domed or cone-shaped roof formed by flat stones gradually corbelled out, but most are square and are more regularly roofed with either turf or stones set in lime mortar, the underside being lime plastered as a precaution against fire.

The Pigsty

Until around the middle part of the eighteenth century pigs were normally kept in the open and were allowed to roam free, especially in wooded areas, where they could forage for food. The passing of the first Enclosure Act in 1750 started a fundamental change in the way that land was farmed and in land rights and the law of trespass. As a result, farmers were obliged to keep pigs in compounds and soon afterwards came the pigsty. From this time onwards keener interest was given to selective breeding and the economic benefits this could bring. The large piggeries of today are very much in contrast to the small low-level structures that were usually seen close to the farmhouse in earlier times. They took the form of a small box-like building to which was attached a confined low-walled area with a chute at one end that discharged into a trough. This enabled food to be passed through at any time, without disturbing the pigs. Poultry-keeping was sometimes coupled with pig-keeping, with a chicken loft being provided immediately over the sty.

The Oast House (Hop Kiln)

The areas of Kent, East Sussex, Herefordshire and certain parts of Surrey and Worcestershire are noted for hop growing. At one time crops had to be dried in kilns at source before being taken to the brewer, and in many areas the distinctive shape of these kilns is a particular feature of the landscape. The subsequent industrialization of brewing has made most redundant, and large numbers are now being used for other purposes. The early kilns were square but aerodynamic theory in the 1800s indicated that better air flow could be achieved with a circular kiln. The idea took hold in Kent and gradually infiltrated elsewhere. The circular shape was more difficult to build and, as doubts grew over the claimed benefits, many hop growers returned to the square form in the latter part of the nineteenth century and the first quarter of the twentieth century.

Built of brick, the kiln had a furnace room on the ground floor, over which was an open slatted floor covered in stretched and tacked horsehair cloth. Until the late 1700s flues were usually made of lath and plaster, but after that time the use of brick became universal. From eave level the shape was reduced upwards to a pyramid or cone that terminated with a revolving cowl set against the wind by a projecting vane. The earlier kilns were open fired, using wood and charcoal, but when coal became cheaper and in general use, it was necessary to isolate the hops from the smoke and flue gases to prevent them being tainted. The trunking was arranged to ensure that the hot flue gases passing from the furnace adequately heated and dried the hops (Fig. 12).

THE MALTING KILN

Malt is an essential ingredient for the brewing of beer and is made from barley. Most malt kilns are found in the hop-growing regions of the country but – as with many other products – the process has become industrialized and is no longer a part of farming. Malting houses are long rectangular two-storey buildings with a kiln located at one end (Fig. 12). The process began with the barley being soaked in water and when it was saturated it was spread out thinly and evenly over the floor of the germinating chamber on the first floor. It was left until the barley had begun to germinate and then transferred to the kiln drying floor. This had open battens covered with either wire gauze or specially made perforated tiles. On completing the process the malt was bagged and made ready for use.

THE DOVECOTE

At one time it was commonplace for farms to feature a dovecote, as the doves or pigeons provided a useful source of meat (Fig. 13). It was something that did not come about until the 1600s, for in the medieval period the installation of a dovecote was a privilege granted only to barons, abbots and lords of the manor. Later, the concession was extended to parish priests. Whilst dovecotes of many different shapes and architectural styles can be found, they all share the same fundamental form, being tall and almost windowless, and most have a series of external ledges upon which the birds can rest. Access for the birds was either through a lantern at the apex of the roof or through high-level openings in the walls or the gable ends. All these

12. Oast house and malting house

13. Dovecote

openings had moveable shutters that could be closed to trap the birds for culling.

The Internal Arrangement
The inside of the dovecote was arranged as a series of dimly lit horizontal rows of small wall recesses extending around the perimeter in which the birds could roost and nest. Placed in tiers immediately above each other, they extended from the ground to roof level. Sometimes the recesses had projecting ledges upon which the birds could alight. Human access to the nests was by way of a structure known as a potence, which had a stout central pole that moved on pivots. Extending from this were arms with ladders attached. The whole assembly could be worked or rotated to give easy access to all the nesting boxes. Apart from the birds being an additional source of meat, the eggs were considered a delicacy and the guano dropped by the birds provided a strong and enriched manure for field crops.

THE ICEHOUSE
Before the introduction of mechanized refrigeration, icehouses provided the only suitable means of storing perishable foods. Most were heavily insulated structures set into the ground in bunker form, in which a cool and constant temperature could be prolonged and sustained (Fig. 14). The ice was either collected and stored during the winter frosts or imported in large blocks from Norway. When ice is packed in volume it melts slowly, and the frozen state could be extended by treating with a freeze mixture – most often a solution compounded from a combination of ammonia, chloride and potassium nitrate, which enhanced the durability of the ice crystals.

The origins of this method of food storage date back to the 1600s, when it was used extensively by the large country estates, but some were constructed for commercial purposes and a limited number were built for communal use. They are more likely to be found in a north-facing location sheltered by trees and overgrowth, which provided additional insulation from the warmth of the sun. Sometimes families with means built extravagant architectural edifices over and around an icehouse as an overt expression of wealth.

14. Icehouse

BEE BOLES, BEEHOUSES AND BEE GARTHS

In the past, bee-keeping made an important contribution to farming incomes and for a long period honey was one of the few available sweet foods. It was also the main ingredient for the brewing of mead, with the beeswax being used for candle making and a variety of other purposes. Bees were originally kept in conical wicker containers known as skeps, which were covered with a mixture of clay and dung. They were subsequently made from coiled straw until the present-day movable bee hive appeared in the mid-nineteenth century. In the summer months the skeps were placed

15. Bee bole

in recesses known as bee boles in boundary walls (Fig. 15), or in niches in the thickness of the wall of the farmhouse. They are seldom found in isolation and collectively are mostly spaced about 2'6" (76 cm) apart.

Identifying Features of Bee Boles
The identifying features of these niches are location and size, but there are regional variations. The dimensions are usually some 12" to 24" (30–60 cm) in width and around 18" to 25" (46–64 cm) in height. The depth from front to back can vary from about 14" to around 22" (36–56 cm). Not only were bees an important element in farming, but they were also used in abundance by the manor and great houses. They are mostly found in sheltered walling with a southern or south-eastern aspect and were especially popular during Tudor times. Records show that they existed in the early fourteenth century and they probably have much earlier origins.

16. Winter bee house

High-Walled Areas
Where they appear in high-walled gardens these recesses are more correctly described as bee garths and are more often tiered. They are mostly found placed some 24" to 36" (60–91 cm) above ground, but recesses of similar dimensions were sometimes made for keeping falcons. In a natural habitat the birds prefer high places so a falcon niche is likely to be at a much higher level. Some of the manor and great houses hosted intensive methods of bee-keeping by housing large numbers of skeps in specially designed summer houses that frequently featured highly artistic latticework and other decorative embellishments.

Winter Storage
During the winter months it was the practice to keep the bees in purpose-built winter quarters, usually identifiable as small square-shaped windowless outbuildings with exceptionally thick walls (Fig. 16). This gave improved insulation and helped to maintain equable temperatures during the critical periods of winter frost. The development of sugarcane plantations in the West Indies and the later discovery of processing sugar from beet around the time of the Napoleonic wars diminished the demand for home-produced honey and bee-keeping gradually went into decline.

THE LONGHOUSE

A longhouse is an early type of building that has living accommodation and an adjoining byre for animals, with a through passage separating the two sections. This form of construction has early origins but most surviving examples were built between the eighteenth century and the latter part of the nineteenth century. They are more usually seen in locations where a natural feature in the ground enables soil from the animals to be drained well away from the living area. They are a particular characteristic of the countryside in north-east Yorkshire and parts of Cumbria and are also found in the south-west and occasionally elsewhere (Fig. 17).

THE LAITHE HOUSE

Laithe is an ancient term for barn, and a laithe house is one where living accommodation and a barn are adjoined in a single structure and have the same roof height. A laithe house does not, however, connect internally with the barn – which is the key difference from the longhouse. It is a type of building that is almost exclusive to the Pennines in Derbyshire but can sometimes be found in the nearby regions of Lancashire (including the outer parts of Greater Manchester) and South Yorkshire. Most were built between the middle part of the seventeenth century and the latter stages of the nineteenth century (Fig. 18).

17. Longhouse

18. Laithe house

Early Farm Implements and Appliances

Ploughing
The earliest known tool for tilling was the ard. The plough developed from this and underwent a number of innovations and changes before reaching the stage shown in Fig. 19. This portrays a typical horse-drawn plough of the type used in the nineteenth century.

19. Ploughing tools: *left* – ard; *right* – plough

Early Harvesting Tools
Until the nineteenth century the sickle was the most widely used tool in England for cutting cereal crops. It had saw-teeth on the underside of the blade, which meant it did not require sharpening. In the southern regions of England the bagging hook replaced the sickle from the middle of the nineteenth century onwards. Whilst the scythe has very early origins, it was not used extensively for harvesting until the nineteenth century. The flail was used for threshing in the barn (Fig. 20).

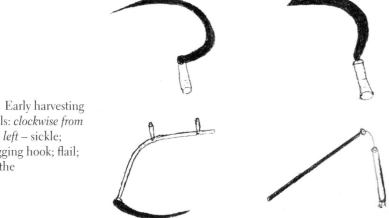

20. Early harvesting tools: *clockwise from top left* – sickle; bagging hook; flail; scythe

The Smock

During work the smock was used as a loose protective outer garment, but as farm mechanization developed in the Victorian period the use of the smock steadily declined. Apart from being unsuitable for the changing methods of operating, it became a hazard and was liable to be caught in machinery (Fig. 21).

21. Agricultural labourer in Norfolk 'slop' or smock, c. 1870 (courtesy of Museum of English Rural Life, University of Reading)

For a selected list of centres that exhibit historical farm buildings and methods see Appendix A.

~ MILLS: THE USE OF WIND AND WATER POWER ~

WINDMILLS

Windmills first appeared in England in the twelfth century and gradually evolved into three basic types: the post mill, the tower mill and the smock mill (Figs 22, 23, 24 and 25). The post mill is timber framed and clad and has a massive central oak post on which the body of the mill can turn into the direction of the wind by means of a tiller or tailpost. The whole rests on a brick base termed a 'roundhouse' that helps to raise the overall height and provide space underneath for storage. The early sails were covered in canvas and were replaced around the latter part of the eighteenth century with moveable shutters that gave the miller much greater operating control. The shutters worked along lines similar to the way louvre window blinds work.

The tower mill is a larger and more substantial structure in brick or stone. The nature of the construction enables it to be built to greater

22. Post mill

(Overleaf) left: 23. Tower mill; *right*: 24. Smock mill

heights and to intercept winds that are likely to be of a greater velocity and strength. Constructed to a battered (inward-sloping) profile for improved stability, the sails connect to a rotating cap and shaft, which link to a series of gears and drive mechanisms that transmit energy and power down to the grinding stones. Most caps are fitted with a device called a 'fantail', which automatically keeps the sails in the direction of the wind. Alternatively, the cap would be turned into the wind by using a system of pulleys or by a pole-type tiller. Mill cap shapes vary in certain parts of the country, with dome shapes being prevalent in Cambridgeshire and Suffolk and pointed arch designs being more of a feature in Norfolk.

The smock mill is very similar to the tower mill; the difference is that the tower is built of timber in the smock mill. Other aspects of the design remain basically the same, including a brick-built roundhouse underneath. Whilst windmills are immediately associated with grinding corn some were also built to work water pumps and they are always found in locations that can take full advantage of the prevailing winds.

25. Mill interior

WATERMILLS

The Variety of Applications

A watercourse with a constant and adequate flow is usually a more reliable source of energy than wind power, which is why watermills are more likely to be found in certain parts of the British Isles. In addition to grinding corn they were also built to pump water, and during the early part of the Industrial Revolution water power was regularly harnessed for metal working and in some manufacturing processes. For a long period the wheels and paddles were wood, but, as metal-working techniques improved, a mixture of metal and wood became the fashion, and from the latter part of the eighteenth century onwards metal predominated. The motivating operation involved impinging a quantity of water of sufficient weight and velocity on to buckets or paddles in a manner that gave continuous momentum and adequate operating power. The mill buildings were mostly built of brick or stone although timber framing with weatherboard cladding was also used (Fig. 26).

26. Watermill

Maximizing the Natural Energy Input
In order to achieve the benefit of maximum power the natural flow of water had to be intercepted in a manner that did not waste energy, and various water wheel designs evolved to meet that need. Water hitting the overshot wheel impinged on the blades at the wheel top, which caused rotation in the opposite direction to the flow of water (Fig. 27a). The pitchback wheel is of a similar design (Fig. 27b), but the blades are set to receive the waterflow at an angle that turns the wheel in the same direction as the watercourse. The undershot wheel allows water to impact near the base, whilst the breastshot wheel intercepts the watercourse half-way up (Figs 27c and d). In waters that are shallow and fast moving better efficiency could be gained by using the horizontal clack wheel (sometimes termed a Norse wheel) (Fig. 27e).

For a selected list of mills to visit see Appendix I.

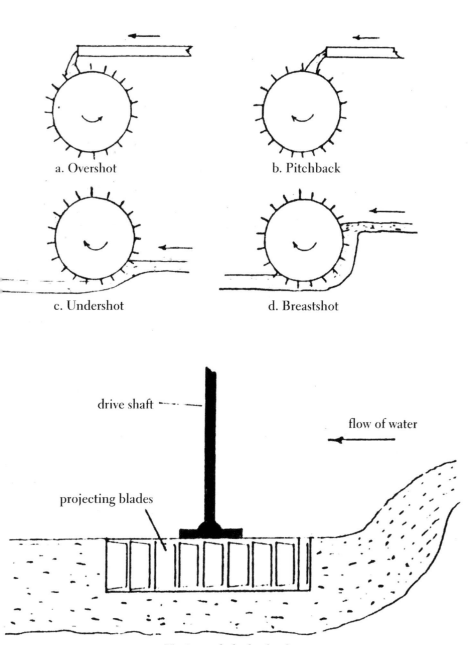

a. Overshot

b. Pitchback

c. Undershot

d. Breastshot

drive shaft

flow of water

projecting blades

e. Horizontal clack wheel

27. Water wheels

28. Lime kilns

4 Industry in the Countryside

LIME KILNS

Lime has been used in Britain since Roman times and formed the basis of building mortars until Joseph Aspin patented Portland cement in 1824. From the sixteenth century onwards it was also used extensively in farming as a soil improver. As a result, a thriving rural industry evolved in the limestone regions of the English countryside. Most surviving examples are in a ruinous state and date from between 1750 and 1850. Whilst there are a number of different kiln designs, those in rural areas are more likely to be in the form indicated in Fig. 28. The various types share some common features and are mainly identifiable by having an arched recess or a series of recesses that are always uniform in size and are about the height of the average man. At the back of the recess is a small arched hatch termed a 'draw-hole', from where the finished product could be extracted.

For a selected list of lime kilns to visit see Appendix B.

POTTERY KILNS

The Staffordshire region has long been the main centre of the UK pottery industry, and the bottle-shaped kilns shown in Fig. 29 once dominated much of the skyline. Innovation and technical advancement have altered the manufacturing process, leaving some of the original bottle-kilns as features of historical interest. Similar kilns are to be seen in other parts of England, such as Cumbria, where suitable deposits of clay were readily available.

For a selected list of pottery kilns to visit see Appendix J.

29. Pottery kiln

COTTAGES WITH WORKSHOPS

Before being overwhelmed by the volume and capacity of expanding factory production, a number of cottage industries thrived in the rural areas close to the conurbations from the middle of the eighteenth century onwards. Buildings appeared that combined a workshop and home under one roof (Fig. 30). They were especially prevalent in the industrial areas of the north-west and north-east and the midland regions of England, but most have now been converted into living accommodation. Whilst the size and style of these buildings may vary, most share a generous range of window lights to the workshop areas, which clearly distinguishes them from buildings with other uses. In the Pennines the windows became so distinctive they were described as 'weavers' windows'. Most of these buildings were used for either handloom weaving, making knitted goods, shoes, rugs or mats

(Facing page) 30. Cottages and combined workshops

31. Spinning gallery

and for wool-carding (carding is a wool-combing process). In other districts similar activities were undertaken as a means of adding to the farm income. In many regions there was a strong emphasis on a certain trade or skill, such as the making of cutlery around Sheffield and the production of lace in the Nottingham area. A few workshops producing some of these items by hand can still be found. The illustration in Fig. 31 shows a spinning gallery attached to a barn.

BUILDINGS CONNECTED WITH COALMINING

Coalmining was once a major industry in Britain, with the larger coalfields in England being located in the north-west and north-east and in the midland counties of Staffordshire, Derbyshire and Nottinghamshire. Important seams were also worked in Leicestershire, Shropshire and Warwickshire. Dependency on coal has now declined to a fraction of the original demand, and huge numbers of mines have closed. Many of the old rural pitheads are still standing and some have been reclaimed for other uses (Fig. 32). As relics of the past, a selected few now receive statutory protection as part of the history and heritage of the areas they once served.

32. Headstock to a coalmine

BUILDINGS LINKED WITH MINING FOR ORES

Scattered around some areas of England are the remains of worked-out mine shafts, most of them connected to the lead industry. In the majority of cases the engine houses and chimney shaft have survived the longest and are still a feature in the local landscape. This is particularly so in Cornwall, where lead-mining was an important part of the economy. Much of the mining was in the coastal regions, and workings often went under the seabed. The familiar circular stone chimney shafts are still a notable characteristic in some parts of the Cornish countryside. The Matlock area of Derbyshire was also a major centre for lead-mining and smelting. Most remaining shafts in this region contrast with those in other parts by their angular shape (Fig. 33).

For a selected list of mining museums to visit see Appendix D.

33. Engine house and chimney shaft

BLAST FURNACES

Iron-working occurred wherever suitable deposits of ore existed, with the earliest form of production being from a clay-built structure called a bloomery. Fired by charcoal, the intensity of the heat was increased by the use of manually operated air bellows; the first charcoal-fired blast furnace appeared in the fifteenth century. Many blast furnaces were eventually converted to coal burning. In 1709 Abraham Darby introduced firing with coke, which overcame the problem of excess sulphur emissions from coal during the smelting process, which depleted the quality of the iron. Few indications of earlier iron-working now remain in the countryside, but a small number of blast furnaces are still standing, most conforming to the angular design shown in Fig. 34.

For a selected list of blast furnaces to visit see Appendix K.

GUNPOWDER PRODUCTION

During the middle of the sixteenth century the production of gunpowder became widespread in England; apart from the obvious military needs, it was also in much demand for the mining and quarrying industries. Gunpowder was compounded from a mixture of sulphur, charcoal and potassium nitrate, from a formula that had originated in China during the ninth century (potassium nitrate is often called saltpetre or nitre). When ground conditions are damp, potassium nitrate can form from decaying organic matter: the mineral nitrates in the soil combine with the potassium content in rotting organic material to form potassium nitrate. After being in solution with water in the ground, the salts eventually evaporate out as potassium nitrate deposits on the surface. Being drier than the surrounding external ground, the earth flooring in many of the buildings of the time provided a wick-like action for the accumulation of these salts. Moreover, if left to putrefy, food or drink spilt during cooking or eating also helped towards the formation of saltpetre. The government made full use of this source during the sixteenth and seventeenth centuries when a regular supply of saltpetre became difficult to maintain. Specially designated government officials were given the power to extract earth floor toppings from any place of their choosing. They often ravaged homes and workplaces by tearing up floor surfaces without restitution. The saltpetre man was a most hated figure and caused much resentment and bad feeling.

For a selected list of gunpowder museums to visit see Appendix L.

34. Blast furnace

Toll Cottages

In order to raise funds to maintain and improve public highways, toll charges were instituted from around 1663 onwards. Between 1750 and 1850 a network of turnpike trusts had been created with the authority to impose charges for the use of designated roads. The trusts were also empowered to erect barriers across the highway in the form of either gates or a turnpike (a spiked barrier) to ensure proper control. At each point of payment a cottage was erected for the resident gatekeeper and, whilst most have since been lost through road widening and other reasons, a limited number are still standing.

The Original Structures
The original cottages were small and basic, and few have survived without alteration or extension. This may sometimes explain why a cottage in a seemingly unlikely and illogical location fronts directly on to the highway verge. Turnpikes were usually placed 3 to 5 miles apart and, by the middle of the nineteenth century, they were unable to cope with keen competition from the railways and waterways. As a result, they steadily became unsustainable and by the late 1870s most had been disbanded. A toll cottage typical of the type seen in the south-east of England is on view at the Weald and Downland Open-Air Museum at Singleton, near Chichester, West Sussex (see Appendix A).

Railway Stations

The Early Shelters
When the first stages of a national rail network began in the early 1800s the rural stations and halts had meagre timber-framed shelters with little regard for appearance or cheer. As the rail system progressed, keen competition began between the various railway companies, who vied with each other over claims of service and passenger comfort. Most also recognized that they could create an impression of reliability and substance through the medium of fine architecture. As a result, some of the leading architects of the time were commissioned to produce in-house styles that could differentiate a particular company from the others.

The Variations in Style

All this produced wide variations in railway architecture throughout the country, and it also started a perceptible improvement in travel facilities. It marked the start of the appearance of waiting rooms with fireplaces, canopied platforms, ample seating and toilet facilities. In the 1960s a large number of rural lines were closed down and the station buildings became redundant. Most have since been adapted for other uses but the original function is still clearly discernable in many cases. A typical country station is shown in Fig. 35 but there are many other variations to be seen.

35. Rural railway station

5 Schools in the Countryside

Education for the Masses

As far back as the 1780s, efforts were made to provide a universal system of education, but at the time the problem was the need for children in poor families to work to sustain even the most basic of necessities. Sunday schools played a vital role in fostering change by teaching both numeracy and literacy as well as religious education. Further progress was made with the provision of charity schools, and in 1808 Joseph Lancaster formed the educational foundation known as the Royal Lancastrian Society.

Under the direction of central government, a system of formal primary education began in England during the early 1800s. Later, the idea of teaching working-class children to read and write was enthusiastically promoted by other charitable institutions, including the Church of England, the Wesleyans and the Roman Catholics. Many other organizations followed, and by 1900 a basic education for everyone was considered essential for the future prosperity of the country. In around 1860, school-building grants became available from public funds; accommodation standards improved following the requirement to submit plans for approval before commencing work. Many of the design requirements imposed then are still relevant in the present day.

Building to Standards

A building had to be rectangular and to be clean, light, dry and airy, and to have toilet accommodation. The effect was to create a regular design with large high-level windows at the back of the classroom and a series of tall rectangular ventilating windows in the walls either side. The sill heights were set at a level that obliterated the outside view when seated. Most schools had a bellcote, and a number were provided with folding partitions that enabled the school to be broken up into small classes when needed.

Most often sited close to the parish church, some schools also had a house adjoining for the headteacher. Many of the early village school buildings have now been either altered or demolished, but some have survived, although few have an educational use. The school in Fig. 36 has recently been refurbished, but the basic design features have remained unaltered.

36. School

6 Churches, Abbeys and Priories

~ CHURCHES ~

Plan Forms

Most historic churches have been built to one of four basic plan types and are either one-cell or cruciform, or have two or three linked but differently proportioned cells (Fig. 37). The original form may not always be immediately apparent due to later alterations and additions. Some of the remaining early one-cell churches narrow slightly towards the sanctuary, whilst the two- or three-cell churches always display a clear physical distinction between the nave and the sanctuary. The Romans were the first to introduce Christianity to England, but after their departure in the fifth century it was eclipsed by paganism and virtually disappeared. It returned in Saxon times through missionaries landing in the north of England from Ireland, and through those directly supported by Rome who settled in the south and built churches in accordance with the Roman basilica style. In medieval times the nave was regularly used for social and other secular activities, which in 1215 resulted in a decree being issued by the Lateran Council in Rome, requiring the sanctuary to be isolated from the nave by an intervening space we now know as the chancel. As a result, more three-cell churches were built after that date, with the chancel being strictly reserved for the clergy.

Following the Reformation, the laity gradually became more closely linked with activities in the chancel and, as time passed, a greater proportion of churches were built to the cruciform plan. Many also had an axial tower over the crossing (Fig. 37d). Notable exceptions were the limited number of circular churches built just before or during the twelfth century. They were originally constructed to serve the needs of either the Knights Templar or the Knights Hospitaller. The Templars had the task of guarding Christian places in Jerusalem, whilst the Hospitallers of the Order of Saint John of Jerusalem provided shelter and care for pilgrims and the crusaders.

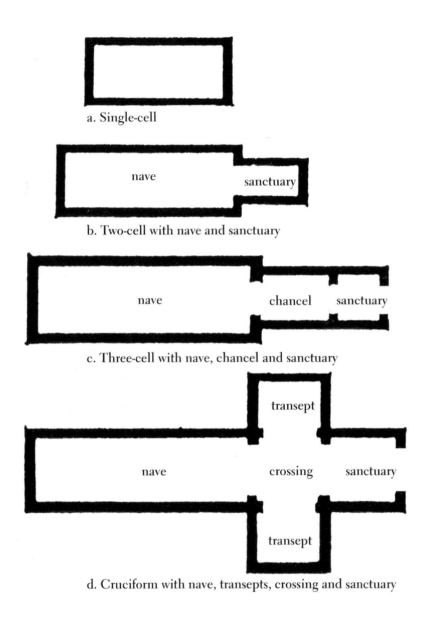

a. Single-cell

b. Two-cell with nave and sanctuary

nave

sanctuary

c. Three-cell with nave, chancel and sanctuary

nave

chancel

sanctuary

d. Cruciform with nave, transepts, crossing and sanctuary

transept

nave

crossing

sanctuary

transept

37. Church layouts. The early Norman churches have an apse at the eastern end in either a semi-circular or polygonal form, but this was mostly abandoned in the twelfth century in favour of the square end.

Until the later stages of the medieval period the nave had no seating, and people either stood or knelt. Some fixed stone seating was, however, provided for the infirm and elderly around the outer walls and a few examples have survived unaltered. It was usual for the Saxons to locate the church entrance at the western end, thereafter it became the practice to have doorways at the northern and southern sides of the nave, a custom that continued until later times. The south door was often made larger and more elaborate and is more likely to have been provided with a porch. Northern entrances in ancient churches are frequently discovered blocked up, from a superstition that evil always came from the north. It is also the reason why the priest's door is found on the southern side of the chancel, and in some churches window openings on the north-facing side were also filled in.

Orientation

The early churches had the chancel pointing eastwards, which is thought to have been a symbolic representation of the direction of the road to Jerusalem. A few exceptions can be found, but the notion also had a practical purpose as this gave the chancel the maximum amount of natural light for the dawn Mass. The practice became an established tradition and is still generally observed.

The Lychgate

An historical feature of interest in many churches is the lychgate, which is a roofed and open-sided shelter placed at the entrance to the churchyard. The term is derived from the Old English word *lich*, meaning a corpse. In the funeral service it was a requirement of the 1549 prayer book for the priest to meet the corpse at the churchyard entrance. This encouraged the provision of shelter for that purpose (Fig. 38).

Chantry Chapels

By the fifteenth century, many churches had chantry chapels. They appear where a priest had been retained by way of an endowment to sing daily Mass for the soul of the provider and others nominated in his or her will. They were mostly a small extension in either the eastern side of the aisle or in the north or south wall, effectively creating a small transept. Some chantry bequests were, however, more modest and took the form of a canopied

38. Lychgate (photograph by kind permission of McCurdy & Co. Timber Restorers, Standford Dingley, Berks)

monument under which was placed a small altar. In 1547 chantries were dissolved by decree, and the space was adapted for other uses.

Underground Accommodation
Some churches have a vaulted chamber placed wholly or partially underground, most often located beneath the chancel. When used to house the tombs of the dead it becomes a crypt, but if the space is utilized for storage or any other secular purpose it is an undercroft.

Ossuaries
Ossuaries or charnel houses are places where the bones of the dead were kept. In the past, a shortage of burial space sometimes meant that graves of

long standing had to be reclaimed for further use. The bones of the original occupants were then placed in an ossuary – either a building attached to the outside of the church or a free-standing structure within the graveyard. During the nineteenth century ossuaries were gradually cleared and the entrances permanently blocked up. Later most were demolished but a few have survived as a feature of the past.

Standing Crosses

Ancient stone crosses positioned near but outside the boundaries of a churchyard invariably pre-date the church and were erected to mark the point for open-air worship. If a church was subsequently built nearby, as a sign of reverence it was usual for it to be so placed in a way that ensured the shadow did not fall upon the original cross. In many churchyards large stone crosses of medieval origin can be found at a prominent point, more usually in a southerly location. They were set up to signify the sanctity of the land on which they stood and were also a collective memorial to the dead (few graves were marked with stone tablets, crosses or headstones until the late seventeenth century).

Church and Community

In earlier times the local lord of the manor, the landowning nobility and the clergy had the influence and power to rule over the people. Moreover, the church was the focal point for community life and was used for entertainment and social gatherings. In the days before the state gave any consideration to organized welfare, the church either provided or created the means by which assistance could be given to the aged, the infirm and the poor. In some localities the nave was also the only available place in which many secular activities could be held. As a result it frequently became a place for trading, legal hearings and festivities, and special ales were often brewed and consumed within the church for important events. Bride ales, Lent ales, midsummer ales and Christmas ales are typical examples. After the Reformation and the growth of Puritanism during the seventeenth century greater deference and respect was given to the sanctity of the church as a whole and uses of a non-religious nature were gradually dropped. By this time the general prosperity of the rural areas had improved, so that most communities could find the means to construct a separate church hall for local events.

SAXON CHURCHES

Throughout the Northumbrian region Saxon churches followed the simple Celtic design, with the walls much extended in height in relation to the size and width of the nave, the length being three times the width. They were also aisle-less and had a small rectangular chancel accessed through a narrow arched opening. It was usual to have the entrance in the north-western corner of the nave. In southern England different proportions applied, with the length being twice the width, and many had an apsed

39. Saxon church

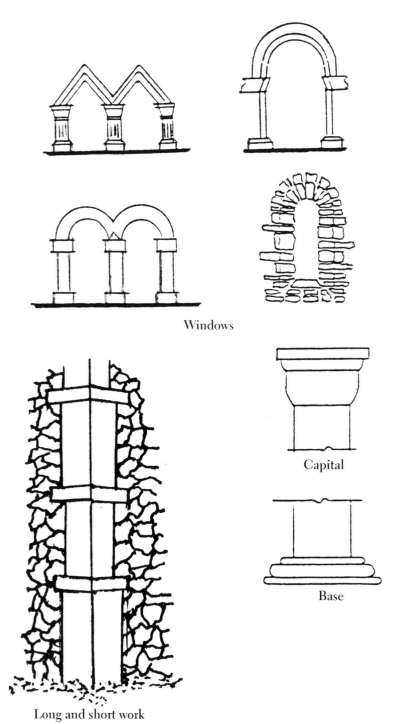

Windows

Capital

Base

Long and short work

40. Saxon church features

sanctuary. A method of shaping the quoins (corners) known as 'long and short work', along with rubble stone or plastered facework divided by pilaster strips, are the more distinctive features of Saxon architecture (pilaster strips are vertical rectangular projections which do not have a base or capital). Also, most window openings have two small juxtaposed lights (window space), with either triangular or half-round arched heads. Larger windows usually have two lights, with a central upright and long and short work at the jambs (the flanks of the opening). Towards the end of the Saxon period Romanesque features also began to appear alongside traditional Saxon designs (Figs 39 and 40).

NORMAN CHURCHES

The Norman Conquest resulted in an enormous cultural change that affected both architectural design and methods of construction. Once firmly established, the Normans embarked on an expansive building programme that included either remodelling or rebuilding many of the Saxon churches, especially the larger ones and abbeys. A large number of surviving Norman churches are two-cell, with the nave a little wider than the chancel, and some have an apsidal (a rounded or splayed) end, as in Fig. 41. This is an item that was later superseded by the square-ended chancel. Many of the more prestigious churches of the time are, however, three-cell, whilst those that have remained unaltered feature wide arched openings to the north and south transepts, with much narrower arches dividing the chancel from the nave and the chancel from the sanctuary.

The Later Changes

In the fourteenth century the constructional definition between the nave and the chancel began to change, with many of the chancel arches being enlarged and separated from the nave by a rood screen (either a carved wood or carved stone screen dividing the nave from the choir and chancel). A rood is the image of Christ crucified – an important symbol of the Christian faith. The cruciform plan became more popular during the later Norman period, and side aisles first appeared at around that time. These aisles arose out of a pressing need for expanded seating and more overall space (the term aisle is derived from the French word *aile*, meaning wing). The present-day use and application of the aisle is essentially a Norman legacy that has had a lasting impact on church layouts and the manner

41. Apsed end to church

42. Norman church

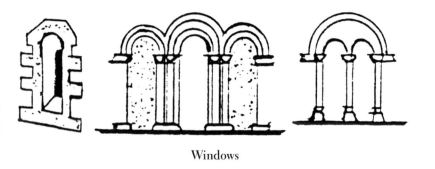

Windows

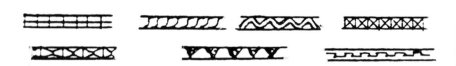

Cornices

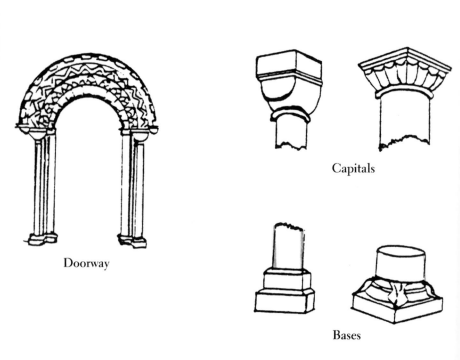

Doorway

Capitals

Bases

43. Norman church features

in which they are used. The elevational style is characterized by walls of extreme thickness and small round-headed windows with deep splays. It was also the custom of the time to feature heavily enriched carvings to the chancel arch and the entrance doorway (Figs 42 and 43). If a church was provided with a tower the proportions were generally expansive compared to the periods before and after.

GOTHIC CHURCHES

The appearance of the Gothic form (Fig. 44) was a move away from conventional mass walling in favour of a new concept. English Gothic passed through four distinct periods of change, which in 1817 Thomas Rickman – a leading architect of the time – grouped into classifications: Transitional (sometimes described as English Romanesque), Early English, Decorated and Perpendicular stages. In practice, mixed detailing will be found in the intermediate phases between the preceding and later styles.

Projecting supports in the form of buttresses were often necessary to counteract the weight of the main structure and to compensate for the weakening effect of door and window openings. Whilst the walls of Saxon and Norman churches had considerable thickness and small windows, additional strengthening was sometimes necessary, provided by buttresses that were shallow in depth but generous in width. The Gothic period that followed this was revolutionary and produced a completely different construction technique. This was achieved through a realization of the scope that the pointed arch offered in vault construction, together with the careful application of deep outward-projecting buttresses and the judicious use of columns and flying buttresses.

A flying buttress is one by which the thrust of a wall is carried by an independent buttress that is connected to the main structure by means of an arch or a series of arches (Fig. 45). What had gone before was a reliance on mass stonework and semi-circular arching, which imposed severe constraints on design and innovation. The dramatic switch to pointed arch vaulting provided the potential for walls to be made taller and thinner, and windows and other openings wider and more expansive. It also enabled internal designs to have greater complexity and versatility.

45. Flying buttress

(*Facing page*) 44. Gothic-style church

The Gothic Phases

EARLY ENGLISH (1201–1300)

The style is more austere than later periods and is characterized by features such as plain ribbed vaulting, plain mouldings with alternate rounds and deeply cut hollows and long and narrow window proportions, with or without plate tracery. Arches are acutely pointed with windows used as single elements or in combinations of two, three, five or seven. Circular

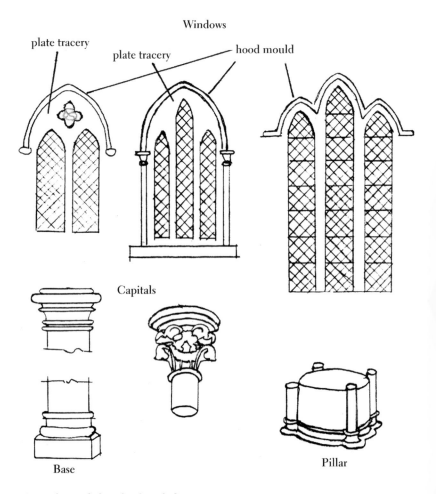

46. Early English-style church features

windows were introduced more regularly in the later periods. Pillars usually have small shafts arranged around a large circular pier. Capitals are generally either plain moulded or have sculpted foliage. Bases are likely to have single or double square plinths. Other notable features are plain hood moulds and dog-toothed or zig-zag carving and outward-leaning crockets (a crocket is a carved leaf-like decoration projecting at regular intervals, most commonly seen on spires, gables and pinnacles) (Fig. 46). Keel moulding is also characteristic of the period.

DECORATED (1301–1400)

A prominent feature of this style is the bar tracery, which is either geometrical or worked in delicate, easy-flowing lines. When pillars are clustered they are usually in lozenge form. Niches are more commonly used and mouldings are mostly formed of shallower rounds and hollows separated by fillets. They are also broader in form. Use of the equilateral arch appears more frequently than the lancet arch in window design (Fig. 47). In the latter part of the period, increased prosperity resulted in more spacious aisles, further refinement and more frequent use of the clerestory

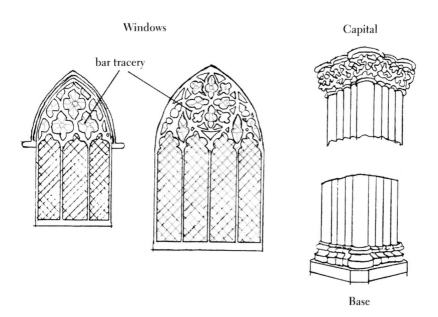

47. Decorated-style church features

(clerestory denotes the row of windows placed in the wall space between the eaves of the nave and the projecting roofing of the aisles below, designed to give additional light). Crockets became inward curving, and ball flower ornamentation appeared. Ogee arches are used occasionally.

PERPENDICULAR (1400–1500)
A distinctive feature of the style is the wide dimensions given to the window openings. A strong emphasis is also placed on vertical lines and the regular use of transoms that cross at right angles in the mullions (a transom is a horizontal piece that traverses a window somewhere between the head and the sill; a mullion is a vertical dividing shaft in a window or panel). In the early stages of the phase, arches are either two-centred or four-centred, and are considerably flattened in later buildings. Mouldings became shallower and more angular, with some in a double ogee or casement form (Fig. 48).

RENAISSANCE CHURCHES
The style passed through transitional stages and in the case of church architecture the Gothic style was never completely eliminated. Outside London the impact that the Renaissance (1620–1820) had on church buildings was minimal as few new churches were needed at the time. Nevertheless, a limited number of churches were built under the Classical influence in some smaller towns and country parishes.

NONCONFORMIST CHURCHES
The main nonconformist denominations aimed for a simpler church design, together with the omission of any form of ostentation or additional embellishment. The elevational treatments are plain and restrained, with little or no stained glass to the windows. This made most nonconformist churches and chapels somewhat inconspicuous and they are not always readily identifiable externally as a place of worship. However, the Methodists did develop a particular style with which many can be immediately associated (Fig. 49), although during the Gothic revival period a number of Methodist churches were built with Gothic features.

Windows, with mullions and transoms

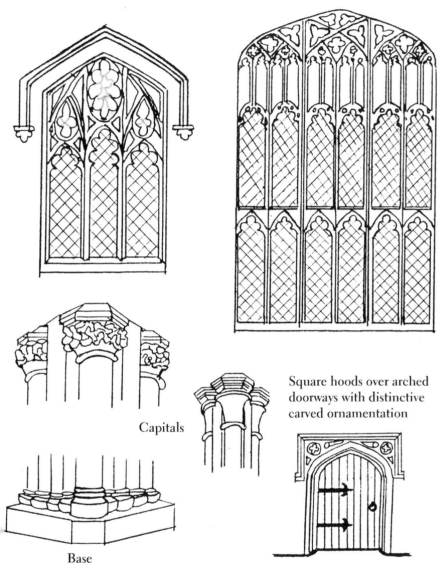

Capitals

Base

Square hoods over arched doorways with distinctive carved ornamentation

48. Perpendicular-style church features

(Overleaf) 49. Methodist chapel

Neo-Gothic Churches

In the early period of Queen Victoria's reign the Church of England was greatly influenced by the High Church movement, which believed that no church could be a suitable place of worship unless the architecture was essentially Gothic. As a result, church building passed through a Neo-Gothic phase (1840–1902) that differed mainly from the original in the indiscriminate mixing of the earlier styles into a single element of architecture without any division, discrimination or recognition of the transitional phases that had occurred in the past. Much of the quality of the work at parish level was poor and lacked the vitality, accuracy and precision of the original. The exception being the work of A. W. N. Pugin and a number of other architects of the time who attained particularly high standards.

Church Towers and Spires

Church towers are usually a dominant feature in the surrounding landscape and more often reflect a particular architectural period, but a large number are later additions or have been remodelled or extended over a period of time. Some of the early towers were detached and doubled as lookouts and as places of shelter and safety from attack. Communities with insufficient funds to finance the cost of a tower usually opted for a bellcote (Fig. 50). A single bellcote placed at the intersection of the nave and the chancel is more correctly described as a sanctus bell, and any tower with a belfry that is either detached or isolated from the main body of the church becomes a campanile. Where the local stone was difficult to work or if flint predominated it was often easier to build towers rounded as this avoided complications at the quoins.

Many of the surviving Saxon and some Norman church towers have either flat-cap or pyramidal spires (Fig. 51). Towers with spires are dominant in Gothic architecture, together with lancet-style arches to the belfry openings and windows. The later Gothic revival followed the same theme as this gave emphasis to the quest for height and the vertical composition of the style.

A spire is probably best described as an acutely pointed structure that extends to a considerable height and serves as a covered roof to a tower or campanile. If the construction between the spire and tower cannot be clearly identified as being in separate parts it becomes a steeple. The early pyramidal roof shape is seen as the forerunner to the tall spire, and – except for the odd variation such as the needle spire and the parapet spire – most of the Early English Gothic spires were broached (Fig. 51). The octagonal shape of the spire was linked to the corners of the square tower by means of an inverted triangular splay. During the Decorated Gothic period parapet spires in stone came into favour, with small flying buttresses frequently being connected to heavily enriched pinnacles. In the Perpendicular Gothic phase the tall spire was often abandoned for either a circular or octagonal drum or a flat roof with pinnacles much extended in height (Figs 52 and 53). After a long pause the broach spire came back into general use as part of the Victorian Gothic revival.

50. Bellcote

(*Facing page*) 51. Church towers and spires

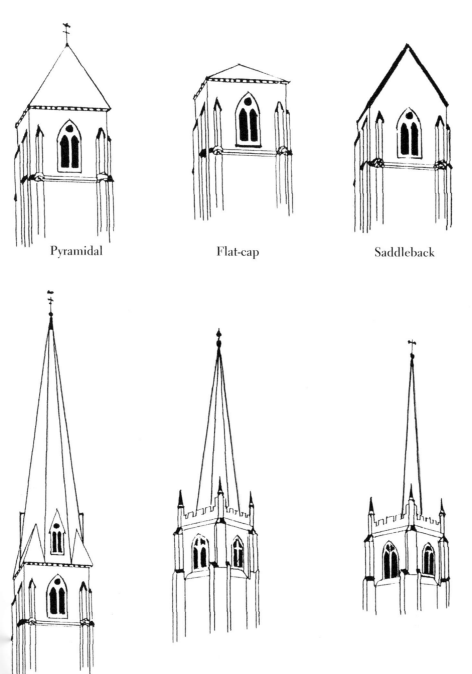

Pyramidal

Flat-cap

Saddleback

Broach

Parapet

Needle

~ ABBEYS AND PRIORIES ~

Before Parliament passed the 1539 Act of Dissolution most of the abbeys in England were major monastic centres and enjoyed a higher standing and superior status to a priory. Where a bishop was also an abbot the community would be administered by a prior and its church designated a cathedral priory. Following the dissolution, a number of abbey and priory churches were taken over by local communities and used as parish churches, which often entailed demolishing parts of the original church to reduce the burden of cost for parishioners. A priory is a religious establishment presided over by a prior (or prioress) and, although of junior status to an abbey (headed by an abbot or abbess), several attained religious eminence and a level of prosperity that far exceeded that of many abbeys.

Deliberate Destruction

The dissolution of the monasteries eventually resulted in a vast number of abbeys and priories being either deliberately destroyed or abandoned and left to decay. In more recent times the monastic orders have become re-established and many have returned to their original locations. Aylesford Priory near Maidstone in Kent is one such example. Founded in 1242, the order returned in 1949 and restored much of the original structure. Visitors are welcome and there are some fine examples of pottery and religious art on display. In 1882 the Benedictine Order returned to Buckfast Abbey in Devon to the site where the early monastery once stood. The monks produce the now famous Buckfast Abbey wine.

For a selected list of abbeys and priories to visit see Appendix C.

(Facing page) 52. Octagonal drum with pinnacles

53. Flat-roofed church tower with pinnacles

7 Castles and Other Fortifications

The Early Castles

After their victory over King Harold in 1066 the Normans consolidated their presence by building a series of castles. They appeared not only in strategic places in the countryside but also in towns, with the specific purpose of imposing strict authority over the local population. Once the new rule had become firmly established, other functions were added to the military role and they became strongholds for a treasury, made convenient centres of administration and provided an imposing home for the local controller. At first the Normans relied on motte and bailey structures using earth and timber. These could be erected at reasonable speed by non-skilled labour and met the immediate needs of the time. The motte was formed from a steep truncated mound of earth, flattened at the top to take a timber tower protected by a stockade, which usually included at least one court or bailey, screened by earth ramparts and palisades.

The Use of Heavy Stonework

By the mid-twelfth century these transitory structures were being replaced by heavy stonework. The timber tower changed to a stone keep and the stockaded ramparts to a stone curtain wall and gatehouse (Fig. 54). This mass of masonry was assembled with an inner and outer wall of stonework filled with a rubble core. The early designs featured a square keep, together with an elaborate array of rooms, featuring basement and undercroft areas, a great hall, private apartments with solars (solar is a medieval term for a private room or bedroom), plus quarters for an armed garrison. Usually the approach was made by stone steps to first-floor level, which for added protection was sometimes linked to a forebuilding. Inner security was also enhanced by keeping the windows small and few in number. The surrounding wall provided a further means of defence with a rampart walk with crenellations, the whole frequently having an added barrier of a moat with a drawbridge at the gatehouse.

Although most twelfth-century designs kept to a square plan, some shell keeps were also constructed in that period. A shell keep is a buttressed curtain wall surrounding a motte, often with the additional protection of a fosse (wide ditch or moat) (Fig. 54). In the latter part of the century, returning Crusaders influenced a change to the Middle Eastern pattern of circular towers. In the early thirteenth century the concentric design began to emerge, with particular emphasis on the defence of the gatehouse or barbican, which was shielded by heavy gates front and back, with each having a portcullis. In addition there were facilities to trap and annihilate any adventurous-minded intruder by way of murder holes and arrow slots for use by guarding bowmen.

The Effect of Increased Prosperity

Increased prosperity during the fourteenth century created the opportunity and scope for improved ideas, and castles became almost impregnable, with higher curtain walls and various different lines of defence. This is in contrast to some earlier innovations that had design faults. Many of the early curtain walls had been capped with wooden boards or screened platforms known as hoardings, but they were highly vulnerable to fire damage from ignited missiles. This resulted in them being superseded by high merlons and V-shaped loops, arrow slots and embrasures for guns and, later, small cannon (Fig. 55). To enable the enemy to be engaged at close range the battlements were machiolated (which meant that the parapet projected over a wall or tower, with openings in the rampart walk that enabled defenders to fire at the enemy immediately below), and more use was made of the bartizan – a small turret projection at the top of a wall or tower that was used as a look-out (Fig. 55).

Modifications Necessary to Counteract Heavier Cannon Power and Stronger Explosives

The emergence of heavy cannon power changed the tactics of warfare and exposed weaknesses in the seemingly impregnable features of the past. The high merlons became prone to damage, and serious difficulties arose in the ability to match an outside attack with equivalent firepower. The rampart walks were too narrow to be used as platforms for cannon – a radical solution was needed. It came with the introduction of the bastion,

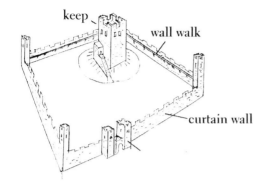

keep

wall walk

curtain wall

Stone-built fourteenth-century castle

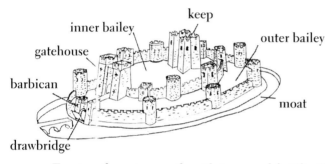

inner bailey

keep

outer bailey

gatehouse

barbican

moat

drawbridge

Fourteenth-century castle with improved fortifications

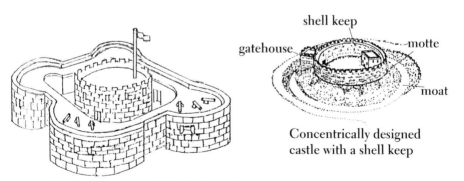

shell keep

gatehouse

motte

moat

Concentrically designed
castle with a shell keep

Castle towers remodelled to form bastions

54. Castle development

Bow

Cross-bow or bow

Hand-gun

Artillery

Loops to fit different weapons

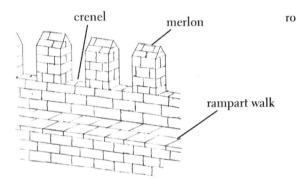

crenel

merlon

rampart walk

Battlements

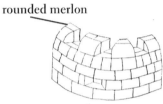

rounded merlon

A later style battlement
with ballistic-shaped
merlons and an
undercover gun port

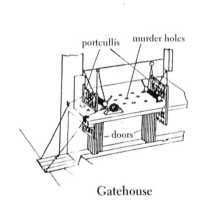

portcullis   murder holes

doors

Gatehouse

Bartizan

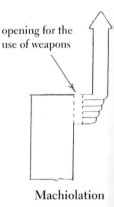

opening for the
use of weapons

Machiolation

55. Castle features

which involved towers and curtain walling being replaced by a completely different structure (Fig. 54). Bastions provided sufficient space and mobility in which cannon could operate. The high merlons of the past gave way to a shorter, thickened and rounded form that had the strength to resist and deflect much of the damage the larger missiles could inflict. Other measures included embanking earth around the lower portion of a curtain wall, which gave added strength and helped absorb the effects of sudden shock and multiple vibrations from gunfire attack (Fig. 56). As the placing of missiles became even more accurate and deadly another latent defect was highlighted. An increase in accuracy enabled attack on 'dead spots' that could not be covered with suitable protective weaponry. Mainland Europe solved the problem by reshaping the bastion to give better protection, but even this needed modification at a later date (Fig. 57). This reshaping is a feature that seldom appears in the British Isles, except in the later fort

56. Castle walling with embanked earth to absorb shocks and vibrations

buildings, a good example being Tilbury Fort in Essex. The absence of this adaptation in Britain is due to the domestic situation – British castles were not at risk of being threatened by invading armies with heavy artillery.

Rounded bastion

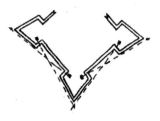

Arrowhead bastion design provides more effective artillery cover

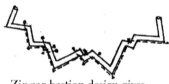

Zig-zag bastion design gives good overall defensive coverage

57. Bastion designs. Dotted lines indicate the line of defending artillery cover, showing that there are 'dead spots' that were not covered.

The Eclipse of Castle Building

The continuing progress in the use of highly mobile artillery and the frightening power and accuracy of gunnery meant large fortifications were no longer suitable means of defence. As a result, castle building went into rapid decline from the sixteenth century onwards. The abandonment of the castle for defensive military purposes changed the emphasis to residential use, though many noblemen and large landowners continued to see them as edifices of authority and prestige.

Gradually, parts of the old fortifications were either demolished, left to decay, or rebuilt to provide improved domestic accommodation. These changes are an expression of the differences in the living styles between the early and later medieval periods. During this time the courtyard house with perimeter walling and a defensive gatehouse won preference in terms of function, suitability and cost, particularly if owners had been given permission to crenellate. This was a privilege granted under licence by the Crown and put the grantee in an ascendant position, with the defensive nature of the layout usually providing the degree of protection needed. This change in emphasis to domestic use is most apparent in late medieval buildings, which demonstrates other changes, including a shift towards the use of brick.

The Effect of the Civil War

The beginning of the Civil War in 1642 created a different climate of need, and fortifications that had fallen into disuse were reinstated. Their susceptibility to fire, mining and bombardment was, however, fully exposed and serious damage was inflicted in a number of cases. In 1649 Parliament ordered some castles to be destroyed and a programme of demolition was put into operation, particularly in the English midlands, Yorkshire, Essex, Surrey, Hampshire and the Thames Valley, the notable exceptions being the southern coastal parts of England, where castles could still perform a useful protective function against a sea invasion from Continental Europe.

For a selected list of castles to visit see Appendix E.

MARTELLO TOWERS

The now familiar Martello towers were built as an additional means of coastal defence against the threat of invasion by Napoleon Bonaparte. Building began in 1805 and by 1808 a line of towers had been constructed from Newhaven in the south-west to Aldburgh in the east. Built in brick, they followed a standard design with a gun emplacement on the roof and an ammunition store in the basement. They were positioned in locations where enemy vessels could be engaged before they had an opportunity to land troops.

OLD HILLFORTS

Scattered around the English countryside are the remains of fortified compounds, many of which date back to Neolithic times (the later part of the Stone Age). Although they are generally described as hillforts, the term is a misnomer, for many are on lowland, but they all shared the same purpose of giving communities and livestock protection against marauders and hostile neighbours. Most are on sites that enabled builders to take advantage of either hilly or sloping ground (Fig. 58). They were created by digging a series of concentric ditches around a central compound, the soil being placed so as to make a range of protective ramparts or revetments (retaining walls). Behind each rampart was a walkway termed a 'berm' that gave easy access to any part of the fort that was under attack. The final line of defence before entry had a ditch and a steep earthbound rampart on which stood a wooden stockade.

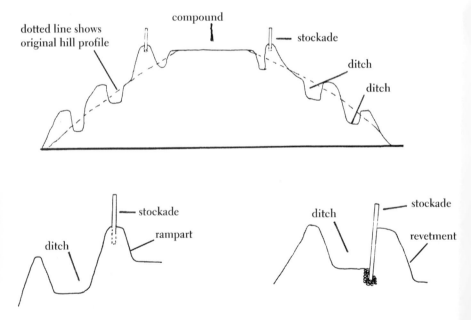

58. Cross-section of a hillfort, showing (*bottom left*) a rampart and (*bottom right*) a revetment

The stockade was formed by either a series of adjoining stakes driven into the ground or a similar pattern of stakes set against an inclined revetment. When the Romans arrived they immediately embarked on a policy of disbanding hillfort settlements and dispersed the population into new and more controllable locations. There is much archaeological evidence to suggest that there was strong resistance to the Roman army. Now part of history, these manmade changes in the landscape have been steadily worn away, but their outlines remain discernable and continue to be an interesting echo of life in earlier times (Fig. 59).

For a selected list of hillforts to visit see Appendix F.

59. An early hillfort, with the earth cuttings still discernable

FORTIFIED MANOR HOUSES (1300–1400)

To be secure, many of the early manor houses needed to be fortified, which required a licence to crenelate from the Crown, and normally this was restricted to those regarded as being totally loyal to the reigning monarch. Enclosure with a high wall enabled a household to be relatively secure from attack or a siege, with many lacking windows around the outer periphery at the lower levels (Fig. 60). A number also had the added protection of a moat, and by making suitable long-term provision for food and supplies it was often possible to survive a difficult period of hostility unscathed.

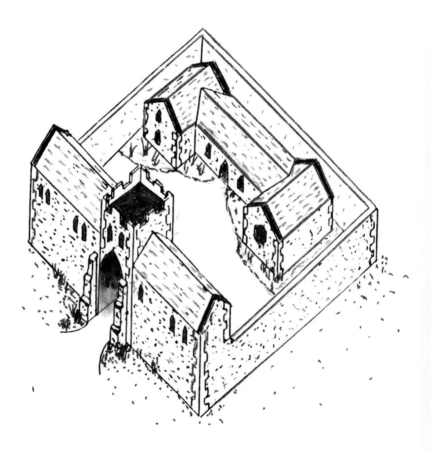

60. Fortified manor house

By the beginning of the sixteenth century the establishment of firm government lessened the need to fortify, and this opened up opportunities for houses to be built for aesthetic appeal and pleasure. This heralded the beginning of an era of building large country houses set in parklands and formal gardens. In the upper echelons of society a keen interest developed in aboriculture and horticulture, and landscape architects such as William Kent and Lancelot 'Capability' Brown prospered, with their skills gradually becoming more widely appreciated. The effect of this change was to alter some local landscapes into carefully crafted vistas of vegetational significance and beauty – the land having previously been used for farming.

Most grand houses also had a growing area enclosed by high and sturdily built brick walling. Known as fortified gardens, these gardens were provided to resist damaging winds and to rebuff rabbits, rats and other animals. In addition, the brick absorbed the heat of the sun during the day and slowly released it at night. The effect was to create a more equable micro-climate within the walled area, making the immediate environment more suitable for the growing of delicate fruits, flowers and some vegetables.

TOWER HOUSES, RAISED HALL HOUSES AND BASTLE HOUSES

In the English regions bordering Scotland and, to a lesser extent, those bordering Wales the way of life was at one time very insecure, and the traditional home often took the form of a defensive tower (Fig. 61). The layout of the accommodation usually followed a regular pattern, with a vaulted and well-protected storage area on the ground floor and the living rooms immediately overhead. The number of storeys varied, but most ranged from two to three and terminated with a battlemented roof.

Another form of defensive design was the raised or upper hall house, which had the ground level again used for storage with the living area immediately above (Fig. 62). Most surviving examples date from around the middle of the twelfth century and appeared at a time when defence had become a high priority. In the thirteenth century the political climate became more secure and the open hall tended to return to the ground floor although the raised hall design continued in a limited way into the fourteenth century and in some parts even into the fifteenth century.

There is a subtle difference between this and the bastle house, where the living accommodation was placed immediately over a stable or cow house (Fig. 63). Apart from being a safeguard against intruders, the body

61. Tower house

62. Raised hall house

heat from the animals underneath helped to keep the human occupants warmer during the winter months. Most bastle houses were built between the mid-sixteenth and mid-seventeenth centuries. They are mostly found in the north-east of England, especially in those areas close to the border with Scotland. The doors at ground level had to be kept heavily barred to prevent cattle-rustling.

63. Bastle house

8 The Way People Lived

The Open Fire
The hearth has been at the centre of domesticity since the beginning of civilization, with the original forms being open and centrally located. When our ancestors moved from caves and other natural shelters to crudely constructed dwellings, the position of the hearth remained unchanged and was a feature that continued in some areas in Britain until well into the sixteenth century. The illustrations in Figs 64 and 65 portray a typical open hall house of the medieval period with a large central hall and an open hearth in the middle of the floor. The larger houses had a dais at one end on which stood the high table used by the master of the household and senior members of his family. A reredos or partition behind the dais divided a solar from the hall (solar is the medieval term for a private chamber). At the far end of the hall a spere (screen) created a passage way that separated the buttery and pantry from the main hall. The buttery was used for keeping beer and other liquids and the pantry for the storage of bread and other dry goods. The larder was originally used for keeping meat.

Ventilation
In addition to shuttered window openings, entrance doors at each end of the passageway could be used for ventilation, and as shelter from the elements, by operating the door that was on the leeward side of the wind. The central hall was always open to the rafters, and smoke from the fire simply drifted up into the roof space and escaped through ventilated openings in the ridge. Although the discomfort of the smoke had to be endured the use of wood as the primary fuel helped to lessen the worst aspects of this. There was also a belief amongst many folk that smoke acted as an antiseptic and helped to prevent disease. It is not uncommon to find soot-stained timbers in period houses as a direct consequence of soot accumulations from an open fire.

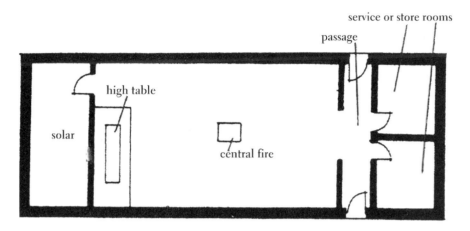

64. Medieval hall house

65. Medieval hall house interior (by kind permission of the Weald and Downland Open-Air Museum, Singleton, West Sussex)

Smoke Bays and Smoke Hoods

The gradual introduction of coal as fuel for the fire started a change in the method of smoke disposal. Whilst smoke from the open wood fire had been acceptable, the density and toxicity of the smoke from coal proved unbearable, and a different method of disposal became necessary. To overcome the problem the fireplace was set against a wall and a smoke bay of wattle and daub (daub is a mixture of earth, straw and cow dung plastered over entwined twigs known as wattles) was built over it; a later development was the provision of a smoke hood and eventually the chimney breast and flue. The large smoke bays and hoods also served another purpose as they were ideal for smoking bacon and other foods.

The Inglenook Fireplace

In the fullness of time, further improvements to the method of smoke dispersal emerged and fireplaces began to have openings with greater depth, height and width. The effect was to create a small room or inglenook – 'ingle' referring to the cheek or jamb of a fireplace, and 'nook' meaning the corner beside it. By this time the hearth was being built of either brick or stone (Fig. 66). In the seventeenth century the inglenook fireplace had become an established feature and changed very little until the appearance of the cast-iron range in the early nineteenth century.

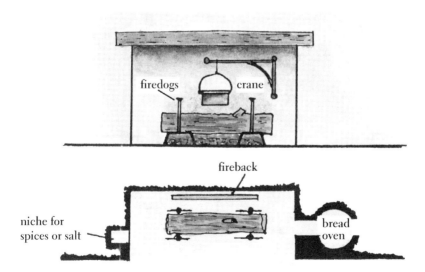

66. Inglenook fireplace

Bread ovens were regularly built into the inglenook and are mostly found oval in plan with a domed cover. To ensure salt would remain dry, many fireplaces also had a small niche for a wooden salt box, which had leather hinges to avoid the inevitable rusting of metal hinges.

By the mid-seventeenth century coal was in common use, which resulted in the grate and firebasket being introduced to improve heat intensity. Andirons and firedogs were unsuitable for coal, and by the late eighteenth century duck's nest grates were being manufactured in cast iron. The abolition of the coal tax was the impetus that thrust coal into becoming the primary heating fuel.

The Slow Move Towards Privacy for the Individual

The early open hall layout made for a highly collective and gregarious existence with little or no opportunity for solitude. The first hint of change came with the more frequent use of the loft space over the solar and service areas for sleeping. It marked the early beginnings of the master bedroom, which later often included a garderobe (an ancient closet). The smaller houses followed the same design but in a more frugal form. From around 1600 onwards the general desire for privacy became stronger, and first floors were either inserted over the open hall area or provided in new buildings to give additional bedroom accommodation. Gradually fireplaces appeared in more than one room and by 1750 most regions of the country had developed an internal layout more akin to the patterns used in the early part of the twentieth century.

The Small Cottages

Early single-storey rural cottages were cramped and restricted in space and most were single roomed; only a limited number had more than two rooms. In certain areas the central hearth with a stone reredos continued, despite the confined nature of the accommodation (the reredos was a low stone screen placed immediately behind the hearth to act as a draught excluder). Eventually the inglenook type of fireplace became more common, with either a smoke bay (sometimes described as a hanging lum) or chimney over it. A deviation from the basic single-storey cottage design was the crogloft, which usually took the form of one room with partitioning at one end to form a parlour. A ladder known as a 'stee' gave access to the loft space above, which was regularly used as sleeping accommodation. Later, a more advanced design appeared where the main walls were taken above the ground-floor ceiling level. This gave improved height in the roof space, enabling it to be utilized more effectively as an area for sleeping and storage.

The two-storey cottage came into more prominence from about 1770 onwards, and most were semi-detached. In some areas lime ash was used as a material in upper floor construction, giving good insulation, and it was hardened to give high strength and durability. The practice has been traced back to the fifteenth century and continued as a feature in some parts until the eighteenth century. The technique involved laying either reeds or straw across the joists as a bed for a mixture of lime and ash that was trowelled to a smooth finish and left to set and mature. In some districts gypsum was the preferred base material as this gave a faster set.

The Advancement Towards Glazed Windows

In earlier times window sizes were influenced by defensive considerations and the exceptionally high cost of glass. The effect unprotected openings had on the warmth and comfort of occupancy was considerable, the unglazed orifices being known as 'wind eyes' or 'wind holes' – hence the origin of the word 'window'. The openings usually featured diamond-shaped mullions (vertical uprights) spaced narrowly apart in a way that is thought by some to have been contrived to act aerodynamically to help reduce penetrating draughts (Fig. 67). Protection from the elements came from shutters fixed internally on either top-, side- or bottom-hung hinges. Alternatively, they were set into horizontal runners that enabled them to be slid into position. As living standards improved, glass gradually became less expensive and glazed casement windows more the norm.

Sash Windows

The emergence of the sash window in around 1670 was at first confined to larger buildings, where they were known as 'shassis' windows. At this stage the earliest sashes were held by pegs, with the upper lights (glazed windows) fixed, but this changed when counter-balancing was introduced. The sashes produced in the seventeenth century had thick glazing bars with small glass panes. As glass improved in quality and strength, designs changed to twelve-pane windows, later reduced to eight panes. At the start of the Victorian period this altered to four panes, and later to one pane to each sash or casement. The horizontal sliding Yorkshire sash was popular during the eighteenth century and the early part of the nineteenth century,

67. Unglazed window

and often provided a convenient solution in situations where restricted headroom prevented the installation of vertical sliding sashes (Fig. 68).

Throughout the seventeenth century, wrought iron was widely used for making casements. Set either directly in stone or in oak frames or sub-frames, the casements were hung on lift-off type hinges set on pins. The early eighteenth century saw a decline in the use of metal, but during the Victorian Gothic phase cast-iron windows proved popular for a period.

68. Yorkshire-style sliding window

MEDIEVAL FURNISHINGS

Sparse and Utilitarian in Function
For medieval people, with the exception of the wealthy, furnishings were sparse, plain in style and essentially utilitarian. Sleeping arrangements were mostly communal, but the fashion always ensured that the master of the house and his wife enjoyed a degree of privacy. A four-poster bed with curtain screening known as a 'tester' was the recognized arrangement for a married couple. Children in particular often slept on a 'truckle' bed that ran on small wheels and could be stored under the tester during daytime. Before metal bed springing appeared, beds had a network of either flax cord or rope stretched across the frame to impart an element of 'give', and a feather or flock mattress would be placed on top of this. Not everyone had this luxury and many had to be content with a straw-filled mattress.

Heavy timber chests were the main source of storage, but most households also had some free-standing cupboard space. The display of banners and wall hangings in the main hall was used as an outward indication of wealth, with paintings, fine furniture and silverware being used for the same purpose, especially from the post-medieval period onwards.

The high table usually rested on trestles and, whilst chairs would be available, much of the seating was small wooden stools. Due to unevenness in the flooring the stools and chairs were mostly three-legged as this enabled them to be stabilized more easily than the four-legged variety. Until pre-Tudor times most tables were simply loose boards resting on folding trestles, but during the Tudor period this changed to fixed trestles united by a strong brace. Trestles were dropped in favour of heavy-legged tables in Elizabethan times. For all practical purposes upholstered furniture was virtually non-existent until the reign of Elizabeth I.

Artificial Lighting
At first artificial lighting came mostly from dried rushes soaked in fat; candles were unaffordable for most households. Cresset stones were also used, which were no more than a small hollow made in a flat stone, into which oil and a wick were placed. During the eighteenth century the cost of candles steadily fell as a result of the development of the whaling industry. Spermaceti, a white waxy substance obtained from the head of the whale, became the base material for candle making. Eventually a more

standard type of oil lamp became available, in which fish oil could be used. This enabled the cost of improved lighting to be kept low in many of the coastal towns and villages.

Flooring

In the medieval period flooring was mostly formed from a clay slurry mixed with earth which was worked to a state of plasticity and then beaten down, levelled and allowed to dry to a smooth finish. Clay was not always the only constituent and sometimes either lime or gypsum were worked into the mix, which hardened into a more wearable screed. The natural porosity of the material meant it was prone to absorb foreign matter; to overcome this, many local practices evolved, including washing down with a mixture of water and soot, which helped to build up and harden the surface. Sometimes small animal bones were driven into the floor face and levelled by cutting or rubbing down, with the various sizes often being arranged into different patterns. Another technique was to add animal blood to the clay, which not only improved workability but also induced quicker setting due to the congealing of the blood. Used either in the main mix or as a screed, the compound could be trowelled to a smooth finish and then polished with oil to produce a hard shiny surface similar in appearance to black marble. In districts that had ample supplies of stone, cobble flooring was often the fashion. Other areas used pitched stone, in which pieces of stone were rammed edgeways into the ground using a pitching hammer. Rush mats were the only form of loose floor covering until the Elizabethan period, when wooden flooring and carpeting became a regular feature in the more affluent households.

The Early Floor Tiles

The burnt-clay floor tiles discovered in early churches and important secular buildings mainly date from the thirteenth century, including those that were lead glazed, when they are usually either dark red, brown or green in colour. Sometimes they are found engraved with patterns or have designs worked in relief or counter-relief. Encaustic work also began to be produced during this time, which involved inlaying designs with different coloured clays. The original medieval tiles can be identified by a general lack of precision and clear definition and little variation in the restricted range of colours. In the nineteenth century tiles featuring reproductions of medieval designs became the fashion and are readily distinguishable from the originals by fine and accurate dimensions, clear detailing and the wider range of colours involved.

Closet Facilities

The first water closet in England was invented by Sir John Harrington during the reign of Queen Elizabeth I, and it drained directly into a cesspit. However, the general absence of piped water to most households meant the idea could not be advanced further. Up to this time, and much later, closet facilities were by way of a garderobe (a latrine) or a privy (earth closet), the latter usually being located in a small hut (the privy house) in the garden area of the property. No further development was made until Alexander Cumming patented an improved water closet in 1775. This was followed in 1778 with a more advanced design by Joseph Bramah, but both types only appeared in buildings of importance and were flushed by various improvised means.

Wash Basins

During medieval times people ate with a knife and spoon and no fork. The absence of a fork meant they were obliged to eat in a primitive way by gripping and tearing food apart with their fingers. After a meal there was a need to cleanse the hands, and the more prestigious homes often provided the convenience of a laver, which was a simple stone hand basin fixed into a nearby wall. Some have survived to the present day and a similar feature is sometimes found in churches and chapels where it becomes a priscina and was used for washing the chalice.

Cooking

The original concept of the solid-fuel kitchen range dates from the sixteenth century, at the time coal started to be used as a domestic fuel. In contrast to wood, which burns freely on an open hearth, coal needs to be held in a slightly raised container and to have a direct air supply. The free-standing fire basket (or grate) provided the immediate solution, which later developed into the fixed open hob grate. Two plates on either side of the hob grate could be used for cooking and heating water. The next advancement came with the open range, which dates from the seventeenth century. Many of the original designs had movable side cheeks that enabled the width of the fire basket to be adjusted according to need. Open ranges remained popular until the beginning of the nineteenth century, when they started to be replaced by the closed range, which was more economic, more efficient and gave improved manual control.

THE EARLY DIET

The Restricted Range of Available Foods
In the medieval period those with means were able to indulge and eat extravagantly, but the average person lived on a mainstay diet of pottage, a type of vegetable stew. Many of the vegetables of today are very different to those of earlier times, but herbs have changed very little. Now part of our staple diet, the potato originates from South America and did not reach England until the late sixteenth century. Moreover, it took a long time to cultivate a number of our native vegetables to the quality and taste of the present day. Carrots and celery are good examples, with celery (then known as smallage) being used for medicinal purposes only, until a cultivated variety came in from France during the early eighteenth century. Pumpkins and marrows were unknown in Europe before Columbus, and the tomato, which also came from South America in the sixteenth century, was shunned as being a member of the nightshade family. Many leading scientists of the time warned of a health hazard from the fruit, with the scare perpetuating until the mid-nineteeth century.

Pigeon Meat
From the arrival of the Normans until well into the late medieval phase the consumption of pigeon meat was greatly restricted. The building of a dovecote was a feudal privilege granted only to the nobility, lords of the manor and the clergy. Heavy penalties were meted out to anyone caught stealing or killing pigeons. As a result, homesteaders were very reliant on keeping chickens, ducks and geese for a regular supply of eggs and white meat. When the restriction on dovecotes was eventually relaxed few farmsteads were without one. People in the lower social groups often caught birds for food by beating hedges and driving them out of their roosts into nets under the cover of nightfall.

Food Storage
Most households kept flour in a 'boulting', which is a type of chest in which flour could be sieved and stored. Bread and other foods were more commonly kept in a 'bread car', a small wooden box suspended by cords from the ceiling as a means of keeping food out of the reach of vermin.

Until sugar could be imported the only freely available sweetener was honey which was also the base ingredient for mead, a highly popular drink of the time. Once sugar from the West Indies became plentiful it was regularly supplied compressed into the shape of a cone called a 'sugar loaf'. It was the custom to suspend this from the ceiling by means of a cord, and to slice pieces off when needed with special sugar cutters.

If ancient rights known as pannage were held, pigs kept by homesteaders were allowed to roam on common grassland during the summer months and to forage in woodlands in the autumn, which gave an opportunity for a better supply of meat.

The Wider World
Rabbits are not native to Britain; they were introduced for their meat and fur in the late twelfth century. At first they were a great luxury for the few, but, as numbers proliferated, they eventually became another source of meat for the country dweller. The reign of Elizabeth I was the time when spices and other foods began to be imported from the Far East, particularly India. As a result food became more varied and interesting, with spiced dishes becoming popular for those in comfortable circumstances. A particular delight was 'sweetmeat' prepared from meat mixed with different spices which imparted a certain sweetness to the taste.

PARISH ORDER

The daily administration of a parish revolved around the parish constable, who was originally an officer appointed by the manorial court, although during the sixteenth and seventeenth centuries the local church vestry meetings gradually became the governing body. The parish constable was responsible for a wide range of duties, including the collection of rates, the maintenance of the local lock-up, the convening of parish meetings, the supervision of jury service and the apprehension of criminals. In 1894 the powers held by vestry committees were transferred to the parish councils and, as local responsibilities grew, many of the powers held by the parish constable also passed to the parish councils. This included the appointment of petty constables who were responsible for the arrest and punishment of offenders. In a few parishes the remains of the stocks and whipping post fixed to the churchyard wall can still to be seen. Mischief-making women and traders found cheating or guilty of minor misdemeanours were strapped to a ducking stool and immersed several times in a local pond or river. The police forces in England did not come into being until 1856, when a codified form of control and enforcement was passed by Parliament.

69. East Barsham Hall, Norfolk, a Tudor house with crenellated parapets where the beginnings of the Gothic influence are fully apparent (see p. 106)

9 Houses in the Countryside

The Great Houses and Gentry Houses

The Great Rebuild

As living standards increased in the early part of the sixteenth century a period of exceptional building activity took place. The change was mostly the result of a greater demand for farm foods and other agricultural products, which enabled farmers and providers to accumulate capital and expand. This started a momentum that stimulated the rest of the economy. The landowners in particular built either new country homes or substantially extended existing ones. In undertaking new works many were quietly influenced by the Renaissance style of architecture that had already made such an impact in Continental Europe. In the upper levels of society social conduct and etiquette also became more sophisticated and convoluted, and there was a quest for more comfort, refinement and quality.

The Social Order

The order of stratification between classes was strictly observed, and the leading nobility needed to be seen to be living in houses of grandeur and significance, and in a style above that of their aristocratic subordinates and the gentry. The houses they constructed became known as the great houses. The gentry are now placed in a broad social category but the term is more correctly applied to the class of people immediately below the rank of nobility. In the course of time upper-class distinctions gradually became less obvious, with many of the gentry acquiring exceptional wealth. Some were elevated to the peerage. Conversely, a small number of the nobility were eventually overtaken by a group of the gentry, and found themselves living in homes of lesser quality compared to the homes of those they had regarded as socially inferior.

For a selected list of great houses to visit see Appendix H, Part A, and for list of gentry houses see Appendix H, Part B.

~ THE CRITICAL PHASES OF ~
ENGLISH ARCHITECTURE

AFTER THE DARK AGES

The Saxons always constructed houses in wood, and reserved stone for church building, which has resulted in few remaining signs of the styles used in domestic buildings throughout the Saxon period. Archaeological evidence does, however, reveal clear differences between the earlier Roman and subsequent Saxon domestic layouts. The Saxons were dedicated farmers and lived together under one roof in intimate association with their cattle, whereas the Romans sought segregation between different activities. The only reliable surviving representation of Saxon architecture is in the churches (see section on churches above and Figs 39 and 40).

The Normans, by contrast, built mostly in stone, and the house illustrated in Fig. 62 is a good indication of the architectural style of the time. For defensive reasons the windows at the lower level were mostly loops (vertical slots in the wall for air and light), with larger round-headed windows being placed higher up. Most of the ornamentation followed the designs seen in ecclesiastical work (see churches, Fig. 43). Whilst the Norman style continued to retain a strong presence, pointed-arch lancet windows began to appear in larger secular buildings during the thirteenth century, together with pointed-arch door-heads. The occasional introduction of the oriel window (a projecting window supported by either a cantilever or a corbel) also occurred around this time. In general terms, secular Gothic always followed more slowly behind changes made in ecclesiastical Gothic. Gothic architecture, however, never made an impact on the more humble domestic buildings – the exception being in the much later Victorian Gothic revival phase.

HOUSES OF THE TUDOR PERIOD
(1485–1560)

The buildings of this period continued to be in the Gothic form and in substance the architectural features remained unchanged (Fig. 69). In domestic buildings, fireplaces became more of a feature, and a considerable amount of building was undertaken in brick, much of it in pattern form with the windows in worked stone. Window openings continued to be small but where large openings became necessary the Perpendicular style persisted, together with tracery and stained glass. Arches were either four-centred or depressed. In some areas jettied construction became more prevalent; this was a form of building in which each storey projected beyond the one below. The oriel window also appeared more often and in a more intricate form. In districts where timber-framing was dominant the distinctive black-painted beams with whitewashed panels prevailed. It was also the beginning of a time when those with means vied with each other more blatantly to display extreme ostentation, overt extravagance and gratuitous indications of opulence.

Houses of the Elizabethan and Jacobean Period (1560–1620)

After the accession of Elizabeth I to the throne of England the religious turmoil of the time was steadily quelled and the economy revived. The newfound prosperity gave rise to improved living standards and introduced a different emphasis on housing style and design. The fortifications to the early manor houses gradually disappeared in favour of enhancements and alterations that made for more comfortable living. It was a momentous time for builders, and many new country mansions were constructed. In the preceding Tudor period symmetry was starting to be an important factor in external appearance; it then developed as an essential characteristic, even although it was likely to conflict somewhat with the conventional plan form of the average house (Figs 70 and 71).

Conventional Layouts

In buildings of substance the result of these fashions was the establishment of three basic internal arrangements, featuring a hall, parlour (the principal retiring room), kitchen, larder and pantry on the ground floor, the bed chambers on the first floor and the accommodation for servants in the garret (attic area). All this was formulated into one of three definitive plan forms as either the rectangular, L-shape or E-shape style. By this stage the great houses also divided into two distinct forms, being either in the courtyard plan or the rectangular block plan with projecting end wings. In essence the courtyard plan clung to the fortification principle, adapted for visual excellence, privacy and pleasure. The early rectangular

70. Shaw House, Donnington, Berkshire, a Grade II listed house constructed between 1579 and 1582. It is one of the earliest buildings to have been designed and built with a wholly symmetrical front elevation.

71. Parham Park, Pulborough, West Sussex, an Elizabethan house built of local stone with a Horsham stone roof. Note the much increased window area in relation to the wall space and the number of gables. The style marked the transition between English Gothic and the Renaissance.

designs also started with the E-shaped plan but evolved later into the H-shaped layout.

The Long Gallery

During this time the long gallery became a notable extra on either the first or second floor; its main purpose is believed to have been the provision of internal space for various recreational pursuits. In the latter part of the period a new emphasis was placed on the main staircase, which became larger and more prominent, with richly carved decorative embellishment. Important changes in the elevations also occurred, with enlarged windows, intricately worked chimney stacks and the introduction of bastardized Classical elements more often adapted to suit the foibles of personal taste.

BUILDINGS OF THE ENGLISH CLASSICAL ERA
(1620–1800)

Whilst architectural styles gradually moved from Gothic to Jacobean and then to a more Classical interpretation, change only came through the activities and zeal of Inigo Jones. He introduced a new style of Italianate Renaissance architecture which had a dramatic impact. Whilst the Jacobean style he challenged had identifiable features with the Classical ideal, it was nevertheless essentially Tudor in concept. The structures Jones designed set a pattern (Fig. 72) that provided a basis for the work of Wren, the Baroque school and the rich age of eighteenth-century British Classicism. This influence was, however, minimal in the smaller and medium-sized domestic houses until the appearance of the Queen Anne style (Fig. 73). This new style provided a workable solution to the problem of combining comfort and reduced size with the spaciousness and dignity of a Classical design. Built with distinctive sash windows, a hipped roof with deep cornicing or low parapeting to the eaves line, together with dormer windows to the garret accommodation in the roof, the style became popular and the epitome of good taste.

Artisan Mannerism

This Queen Anne style was in contrast to the earlier work of Jones, who screened low-pitched roofs with plain parapets combined with a rectangular plan with no gables or projections. His elevations were

72. Classical house

symmetrical and required unhindered space, which meant they could only be suitably applied to large structures. At first-floor level he introduced taller windows and high ceilings, which gave a strong visual impression of overall elegance and grace. This was also the time of artisan mannerism, a term used to describe a style where the features of Classicism had been used in an arbitrary way. It developed more by contact and the exchange of ideas and was in essence an outcome of the feelings and interpretations of craftsmen who lacked any formal training or adequate knowledge of the rules of Classicism.

73. Queen Anne house

74. Chatsworth House, Derbyshire. The Baroque additions by William Talman conceal many of the original Elizabethan features. The grounds are the work of Lancelot 'Capability' Brown. Close to the house is an extensive water cascade built by the French designer Grillet in 1696.

Buildings of the English Baroque School (1690–1730)

Baroque architecture emanated from Italy, but the true Continental style did not establish more than a occasional presence in Britain. Chatsworth House (Fig. 74) is an example where the Baroque influence is very subdued and may not be immediately apparent to the untrained eye. Many of the palatial residences built during this period are nevertheless in a form of English Baroque, with the principal rooms and formal reception areas arranged as a *piano nobile*. In classical architecture this was the most important storey of a building. It is more usually at first-floor level, with the ground floor being featured as a basement or podium – the literal meaning of the Italian term is 'noble floor' or 'place of the nobility'.

The Changed Approach

The old Classical Renaissance rules were sacrificed to achieve effects of grandeur and complexity. Whilst more restrained than that seen in Europe the resultant style was nevertheless diverse and highly decorated and

75. Castle Howard, North Yorkshire. Designed by Sir John Vanbrugh, the building is a strong and robust presentation of English Baroque. It was the first private residence in England to have a dome.

distinctive. It evolved mainly through the work of Nicholas Hawksmoor (1661–1736) and Sir John Vanbrugh (1668–1743) (Fig. 75). It is characterized by curvaceous shapes and the grouping together of various features, some in bulbous or convex form (a feature known as pulvination). It was still Classical in concept, but the different styles or orders were used collectively and in a more decorative and less disciplined fashion. In the larger buildings many of the principal rooms were oval shaped. In essence the style emphasizes the free use of curves and other features within the framework of the Classical orders.

Buildings of the English Palladian School (1710–60)

After 1730 English architecture began to enter a more sober period known as Palladianism. Whilst Inigo Jones had already fostered the quality of Palladio's work, there was a sudden acceptance of his ideals which became more coherent and compelling and a feature of social value. Again this began with the larger buildings but the style eventually trickled down to smaller houses, especially in suburban middle-class locations. The general interpretation of the style was, however, more individual and selective but it became popular in the building and rebuilding of the larger country houses and mansions.

In basic terms Palladianism meant a return to conformity and the strict rules of ratio and proportion which govern classicism (Fig. 76). Obeying

76. Wardour Castle, Wiltshire. The house is considered to be the finest example of the work of James Paine, a devotee of the Palladian tradition. All the essential features of Classicism are present. The design is symmetrical and the vertical elements are in the correct hierarchical sequence, with the windows above the basement level diminishing vertically at each increase in height. The basement stonework has been rusticated and the centrally placed portico is dominant and suitably proportioned in relation to the rest of the building.

these constraints produced a plainer and sterner appearance but also gave images of solidity and cultural meaning. Houses built in the style invariably had four storeys with rectangular sash windows set vertically immediately above each other. Following modest proportions at ground level the sill-to-head length was greatly increased at the first-floor stage, and thereafter reduced in height at each successive level, with the top-floor windows being reduced to a square. Some important features of Classical architecture are shown in Fig. 77.

Gate Lodges

Landowners realized that a strong visual statement at the entrance to an estate was an important expression of power, wealth and influence. The entrance was also seen as a way of creating a favourable first impression through the quality of workmanship; this effect was achieved by the provision of large decorative entrance gates with a pleasing lodge adjoining. As a feature this was intended to make a very positive initial impact even before

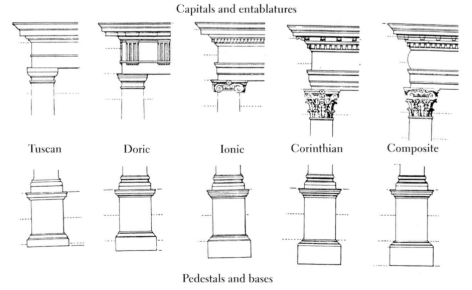

Capitals and entablatures

Tuscan   Doric   Ionic   Corinthian   Composite

Pedestals and bases

77. The Classical orders

the imposing main residence came into view. A large number of these lodges reflect the architecture of the manor house, but in the nineteenth century they started to become the subject of adventurous designs, which at times were frivolous and out of place, with sobriety not returning until the Gothic revival in Victorian times (Fig. 78).

78. Gate lodge

~ Local Building Materials ~

How Materials Affected the Vernacular Styles and the Methods of Building
Vernacular building can be described as the use of materials indigenous to an area, the application of which has been undertaken in a manner not influenced by outside factors or fashions from elsewhere. The outcome is thus derived from techniques acquired by local knowledge, experience and skill passed from one generation to another. Isolation, difficult terrain, unsuitable roads and the cost of transportation all contributed towards circumstances that compelled communities to build in locally available materials. Innovation and adaptation were often the only means by which people could survive and meet their needs; this is why there are many different building methods in the geographical regions of the British Isles. In essence, many of these variations represent an interpretation of a particular need or way of life, apart from the special relationship they share with the materials used and the natural surroundings. In some parts the application of materials will be found to have altered substantially even within small distances as a direct result of ease of supply and ready availability.

Timber-Framed Construction

The Rich Legacy
The use of timber began with buildings of a most rudimentary nature and culminated in a degree of artistry and unparalleled craftwork that endured until superseded by brick and other materials. The Romans, the Normans and the Saxons all used timber extensively, although little tangible evidence remains. The oldest known surviving timber edifice in Britain is at Greenstead in Essex, where parts of the original Saxon walling to the church still stand. This is of particular interest because the Saxons used completely different assembly techniques to the Normans. The carpentry methods used in Britain today are still based on those introduced by the Normans.

Indigenous Oak
The indigenous oak met all the requirements of builders with its strength, quality and endurance, but as the demand for home-grown oak increased, the supply could not keep up, which resulted in a corresponding rise

in price. The dictates of economics heightened as oak became used increasingly for shipbuilding, charcoal-burning and various other outlets. In consequence many builders turned to alternatives such as willow, hornbeam, elm and Spanish chestnut, but only a few properties built in these timbers have survived.

It was the usual practice to erect oak framing from green unseasoned wood, which accounts for much of the warping and twisting seen in so many buildings of the time, following shrinkage from sap evaporation. During the evolution of the timber frame three distinct methods of construction developed: cruck, post and truss, and box frame (Fig. 79), which should be seen as being technically and geographically separate, although these systems do overlap in certain areas. The reason for these regional differences is inexplicable, but the homeland of cruck is essentially in the north of England and Wales, whereas framed walling is almost exclusive to the south-east of England and East Anglia up to about the southern bank of the river Humber. In between are zones of mixed influence in which cruck predominates in some places and framed-wall construction in others. In intermediate zones cruck frames are in the ascendency in the English midlands and parts of the north-east of England, whilst a strong wall-framed presence outnumbers cruck framing in the south-west and mid-south of England.

The Cruck Frame

The reason for the use of the intriguing cruck frame is still unclear and has yet to be accurately deciphered, but even more perplexing is why it should have been adopted for total use in some areas to the complete exclusion of other techniques. The highly innovative thinking behind the cruck frame design has captured the interest of antiquarians and researchers for many years and various theories have been propounded. The debate is still continuing and at one time it was thought the idea came from ship construction (the cruck frame form resembles an upturned boat). Others have been influenced by the notion that cruck framing is Celtic in origin because the cruck principle is also found in Continental Europe and can be linked to areas where strong Celtic influences remained even after the Roman invasion.

The ground-to-ridge type of cruck frame is found in two principal forms: either the closed cruck or the open cruck. Both are shown in Fig. 79 and particular note should be made of the restrictive effect of the closed cruck, which sometimes created a headroom problem but persisted in the north of

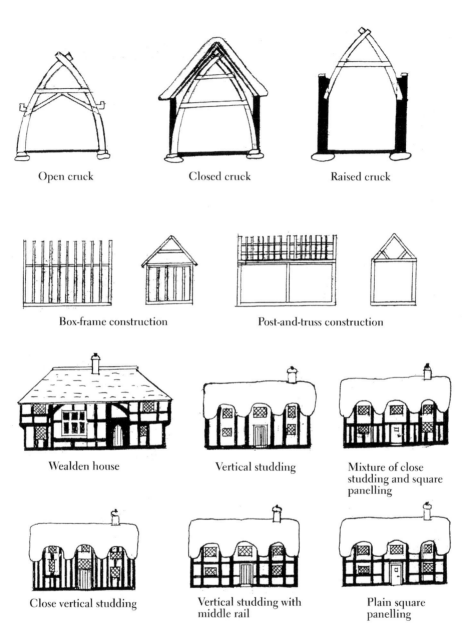

Open cruck   Closed cruck   Raised cruck

Box-frame construction   Post-and-truss construction

Wealden house   Vertical studding   Mixture of close studding and square panelling

Close vertical studding   Vertical studding with middle rail   Plain square panelling

79. Identifying timber-framed buildings

England for a long time. As a result, many cruck buildings in the north are single storey. The open cruck is more frequently found further south and gave added flexibility to the internal layout. The advent of the raised cruck enabled rooms to be proportioned differently in both height and width, including giving better scope for unfettered first-floor accommodation. The component bays used in the cruck regions usually ranged from 12ft to 15ft (4–5 m) in length, with many of the worker cottages being only one bay (Fig. 80). In overall terms the timber dimensions in the early buildings were much thicker and more closely spaced apart than those which came later, due to ever increasing timber costs.

80. Cruck-built cottage

The Post-and-Truss System

The post-and-truss system is basically a series of load-bearing truss frames spaced to form bays. In design terms it is a roof truss resting on sturdy vertical posts with the weight of the roof being taken mainly by purlins (stout timbers fixed horizontally) framed into the roof trusses. The intervening roof rafters take less direct loading, especially where wind braces have been introduced to direct as much weight as possible towards the trusses. In reality this means that the intervening timber walling between the truss frames is little more than infilling.

The Box-Frame Method

Whilst post and truss and box frame may look similar, in structural terms they are very different. The concept for the box-frame technique is a series of uprights that share the roof load equally. Buildings constructed from this method can sometimes give a more refined appearance, although they may be of no lesser antiquity, and clear differences in style can be found throughout the timber-framed regions.

Jettying

Some distinctive variations occurred using the square-framed principle, the more notable being the jettied building, a feature that is also seen in the Wealden houses found in the south-east of England and parts of Essex (Fig. 81). The jetty is that part of the building which projects beyond the rest and overhangs the walling below. The reason for jettying has not been properly identified, and a number of theories have been suggested but not proved. In comparative terms land in the towns was often expensive, and it may have originated as a ruse to maximize site utilization and to create extra floor space. It could equally have been a simple expedient for keeping the lower levels protected from excessive weathering. It is known that in medieval times downpipes and gutters were seldom, if ever, used – which presents a strong case for a system of overhead protection. Nevertheless, it is not a particular feature of rural areas except in the Wealden style of property.

Regional Variations

Other differences in the way timber-framed buildings have been assembled are apparent throughout England, especially in relation to studding and bracing (studs are infill timbers that run the full height of a building to divide a wall into a series of panels). Close studding is where the timbers have been narrowly spaced (Figs 79 and 82). A particular characteristic is the way the studs run full-height without any visible interruption or other sign of strengthening by railing or bracing. This is a notable feature in East Anglia, but from the fifteenth century onwards the style penetrated into large areas of southern, south-eastern and eastern parts of England. Richard Harris in his book *Discovering Timber-Framed Buildings* identifies distinct differences between houses either side of a line drawn from the Weymouth area of Dorset in the extreme south through to Wiltshire, Oxfordshire, Northamptonshire, Lincolnshire and East Yorkshire in the far north (this

82. Restored timber-framed house built around 1250, Suffolk

(*Facing page*) 81. Jettied house, at the Weald and Downland Open-Air Museum, Singleton, West Sussex

83. Timber-framed house, Bolton, Lancashire

follows the central limestone belt). All the counties south-east of this line tend to use the same mode of framing. The counties to the north and west of this deviate from the others by exposing the middle railing (the areas concerned encompass the south-west, the midlands and the remainder of the north). Other variations occur, such as a mixture of close studding and square panelling (Fig. 79). Some regional differences are notable, such as the type of close studding used in parts of Yorkshire (Fig. 83) and the Wealden houses in the south-east of England (Fig. 84).

Square panelling came into prominence in the midland regions around the middle of the fifteenth century, and by the seventeenth century was in general use in many other districts further south, especially Hampshire, Sussex and parts of Surrey, where the plainer styles prevailed (Figs 85 and 86). Curvilinear and intricately worked bracing and decorative infilling is a particular characteristic of the midlands, more notably around the districts

84. The 'bayleaf' house at the Weald and Downland Open-Air Museum, Singleton, West Sussex, which is a timber-framed hall house. Note the jettying to the front and the unglazed diamond-shaped mullions in the window openings.

85. Elizabethan farmhouse, Surrey

86. Timber-framed house with brick nogging and thatched roof, near Selbourne, Hampshire

of Cheshire, Shropshire and parts of Staffordshire. Diagonal bracing is more of a northern feature, especially in Lancashire and Yorkshire. In Yorkshire, closely spaced thick timbers typify the regional style of the fifteenth and sixteenth centuries. During the Elizabethan and Jacobean period (1560–1620), most timber buildings of importance displayed a considerable amount of ornamentation and decorative carving, which gave eye-catching expression to the social and financial standing of the owner (Fig. 87).

87. Little Morton Hall, Cheshire. Built around 1559, the house is a classic example of the exceptionally fine and distinctive timberwork found in the region.

The External Finishes to Timber-Framed Buildings

TRADITIONAL PRACTICES

The open panels within the timber framework were either filled with wattle and daub or brickwork known as nogging, the latter being used at a later date and mostly as a replacement material (Fig. 88). Wattle is an interwoven network of twigs plastered with a mixture of clay, straw and cow dung known as daub. The cow dung was added to give extra strength to the mix and a better degree of protection against penetrating damp. Many timber-framed buildings were rendered in a lime/sand mix but in some parts of England it was more customary to clad with weatherboarding (also known as clapboarding) (Fig. 89). Most weatherboarding styles date from the late sixteenth century and for a long period seems to have been confined to use on farm buildings. All evidence suggests that it did not appear on dwellings until the late eighteenth century. It is a particular characteristic of Kent but is also prevalent in Sussex and parts of Surrey, where it is more

88. Brick nogging

89. Weatherboarding

usually seen applied to the upper levels only. In some areas it was also the practice to coat the timbers with tar. In a number of districts, especially in parts of Essex, the external wall faces to timber-framing have been lath and plastered with a finish of fine gravel. The gravel was thrown on to the wet plaster and later limewashed. This gives a textured surface very different to that found on pebble-dashing.

MATHEMATICAL TILING

An ingenious form of cladding that dates from the end of the seventeenth century is mathematical tiling. Devised to simulate the appearance of brickwork, it served not only as a form of weather protection but also as a means of updating the appearance of a building when brick came into fashion. The tiles were usually hung on boarding or oak or hazel battens nailed to a timber frame. The joints between the tiles were pointed in lime mortar in the same manner as brickwork (Fig. 90). It can be extremely difficult to detect from a casual observation.

Another form of protective cover was slate-hanging, which can be traced back to the early part of the seventeenth century and became popular in

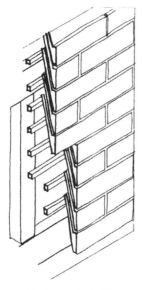

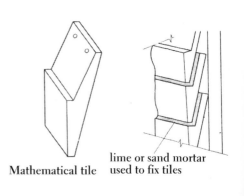

Mathematical tile   lime or sand mortar used to fix tiles

90. Mathematical tiling

the slate-bearing regions of the British Isles. It is now mostly seen in the coastal areas of Devon and Cornwall and in the Lake District.

PARGETING

Pargeting (or pargetting) is a form of ornamental plastering applied to the exterior of buildings and has been featured in some parts of England for around 400 years The medieval plasterers developed the technique into nothing less than an art form and it became a highly individualistic fashion in some parts (Fig. 91). The homeland of pargeting is to be found in the counties of Essex and Suffolk but there is also a strong influence in parts of Hertfordshire, Cambridgeshire, Norfolk and north Kent and it is occasionally seen in other regions. It is more usually associated with timber-framed construction but it is also found on clay lump (described later).

As a decorative style pargeting passed through a number of phases, but in essence it always featured a series of mainly repetitive designs that had been either incised or worked in motifs, swags and relief. When pargeting first appeared it was restricted to scoring designs into the wet render, termed 'stick' or 'combed' work. When raised ornamentation first appeared it started in a restrained form but later became a means of expressing personal wealth and status when designs altered to exhibit intricate and extravagant features. The elaborate pargeting found in East Anglia began during the sixteenth century and reached its artistic zenith around the middle of the seventeenth century. After this the fashion then went into decline but it did enjoy a brief revival around 1900.

For a selected list of places with pargeting see Appendix G.

UNBAKED EARTH CONSTRUCTION

Cob

Generically this technique has become known as cob but the term should more correctly be confined to the counties of Devon and Dorset. In other parts of the British Isles many different local names can be found, such as 'clam' in Cornwall and 'dung' in Cumbria.

The use of cob was generally restricted to the building of cottages, the more humble farmhouses, barns and outhouses, although some prestigious dwellings have been built in this way. In some parts of the British Isles cob remained in extensive use until the middle of the nineteenth century, but

91. Pargeting, Clare, Suffolk

as facilities for the movement of freight improved and the overall prosperity of the people increased, brick and other products began to displace the use of compacted earth. The abolition of the brick tax also acted as a further disincentive to use cob. The decline was gradual, however, and cob construction endured until well into the twentieth century, with the last examples being completed as late as 1925.

SUITABLE SOILS

Not all soils are suitable for this purpose, particularly the light sandy types, and in consequence geology has had an influence on the location of cob. It is found mainly in Devon, parts of Dorset, south Hampshire and Wiltshire and in some localities in Cornwall. It can also be seen in the Aylesbury area of Buckinghamshire under the local name of 'wichert'. Compacted earth building in the form of clay lump was used extensively in Cambridgeshire and the adjoining central areas of Norfolk and Suffolk. A limited amount of cob is also found in various parts of the central midlands of England. It is also present in the northern border regions of Cumbria and can sometimes be seen in other parts of the country where isolated deposits of suitable clay are to be found.

THE BINDING QUALITIES OF CHALK

The longest-surviving buildings are usually from clays that contain a proportion of chalk, which has the effect of binding the mix, resulting in a more durable material. Many of these dwellings are derived from a self-build style of activity, with people in rural communities combining to help one another in the construction process. Site activity always began with the digging-out of a flattened circle of clay, which had to be picked over by hand to remove the larger stones, after which the material would be worked into a heap of about 6 ft (2 m) in diameter. Starting at the edge, workmen then dug over the prepared clay, using cob picks and treading it in whilst water was lightly sprinkled over the surface and straw added. It was considered necessary to turn the mix over at least twice before it was ready for use. The material was worked from a brick or stone plinth (called a pinning) and was built up in layers of between 1 ft to 4 ft (0.3–1.2 m) in depth called scars (Fig. 92). It took about two to three weeks to dry before it was stable enough for the next lift (layer). The configuration of a wall was largely determined by eye, which explains the rather wavy contouring so often seen in these structures and the rounded or near-rounded corners (Fig. 93).

92. Building a cob wall

93. Cob cottage, Devon

Clay lump
The method used in Cambridgeshire involved making building blocks of clay. Prior to moulding, the clay was tempered in a similar way to cob, which included the addition of straw, and after casting was left to dry thoroughly before use. When hard, the blocks were laid in an identical style to fired bricks, using a mortar of either lime and sand or a clay slurry. A major advantage in this technique was in the pre-drying of the blocks, which substantially reduced drying shrinkage. This in turn enabled walls to be built in conjunction with either brick or stone, and a large number of buildings in the region have a brick facing that gives a deceptive impression of the nature of the construction (Fig. 94).

～

Signs Indicating the Use of Cob

~ Presence of a brick or stone plinth around the perimeter of a building (known in Devon as a pinning).
~ Undulating and uneven surfaces to the walls.
~ A large overhang to the roof, which is usually thatch. This is necessary to throw rain away from the walls and prevent penetration.
~ Extreme thicknesses to the walls.
~ Thick lime plaster rendering.
~ The rounding of all corners.

Signs Indicating the Use of Clay Lump

~ Unusual wall thicknesses.
~ The presence of a projecting brick plinth.
~ Brick-on-edge facing.

～

94. Clay-lump walling

10 Building Materials

STONE

The Different Stone Strata

The geological formations in the British Isles are probably unique in containing some remarkable contrasts and variations within a small area. This abundance of differing types of stone has resulted in the creation of a number of individual building styles in the regions (Fig. 95), which today serve as a constant source of visual interest. As might be expected, the principal geological formations mirror a strong presence of stone building in the regions concerned (see 'Building Stones of the Regions' below). The earliest stone buildings date back to prehistoric times, the shape being in the form of a circle, a style that some peasant folk perpetuated until the medieval period. The Romans introduced the necessary skills to quarry and cut stone to shape, but it was left to the Normans to raise the standards to the level of a true craft. The finesse, skill and levels of dexterity that developed enabled stone masons to be highly remunerated in comparative terms and to enjoy an elevated social position. The application of these superior skills did not, however, percolate down to the vernacular scene until into the sixteenth century or in some districts much later.

Dressing and Working Stone

The evolution of stone masonry was a slow development, from the use of rubble stone to roughly dressed and later finely dressed stone that is seen in the high quality and styles we witness in the present day. It was the practice to build in solid wall construction which, if left unprotected, relied upon having a good thickness to help conserve heat from the open fire and to give adequate resistance from penetrating rain. The extent to which these factors interrelate are affected by the manner in which a wall has been built. The various styles of walling are broadly grouped into rubble work – which is the use of roughly broken quarry stone set uncoursed or in courses (coursing is the arrangement of stone in a series of horizontal and regular lines) – or in a form known as ashlar. Ashlar may be either rough or fine work (Fig. 96). The term rough ashlar applies where stones have been cut to a proper finish and are reasonably true and square. In fine ashlar work the blocks have not only been carefully cut and dressed to a particular level of accuracy, but the mortar joints are also exceptionally narrow and uniform. In high-quality work, rustication was often used (where chamfers or squares were formed around the face edges of individual blocks) (Fig. 97). Fine ashlar work was not a feature of vernacular building.

A The Weald
B Wessex
C Cotswolds
D West Country
E West Midlands
F Eastern Shires
G East Anglia
H Lake District
I Northern Counties

95. Map of the different regions of England. The areas marked A to I broadly indicate the different vernacular styles.

96. Ashlar

97. Rustication

The Visual Impact of Shape

When stone is taken from the ground it can be broken into suitable shapes by exploiting the physical characteristics of its composition such as stratification. With random rubble work this not only determines the appearance of the stone but the way in which it is used. Certain stones, for example, break naturally into roughly squared or oblong blocks, whilst others split into elongated lengths, and still others, like ragstone, are totally irregular. As a result, many of the more interesting vernacular applications are the outcome of a complex local geological make-up and use of a variety of different stones. This diversity can include sarsens and erratics. Sarsens are boulders of grey sandstone that appear to have no relationship with other stones in the area. In reality they are the remnants of an original sandstone stratum that has otherwise completely eroded away. Erratics are stones that have been transported to another location by glacier action. Various ways of using stone for walling are shown in Fig. 98.

BUILDING STONES AROUND THE REGIONS

The properties that determine the way stone can be cut and dressed concern the natural configuration, density, texture, hardness, crushing strength and durability. These are all factors that influence the way stone has been worked throughout the regions. The exceptions are the buildings of grandeur, where the stone has often been specially selected and transported from elsewhere.

The Weald
(East and West Sussex, Surrey and Kent)

A sandstone series termed greensand runs mostly through the central parts of these counties and was used as a regular building material. The presence of different mineral salts in the ground has resulted in the colours varying from a greenish yellow or greenish grey through to grey, pale yellow and dark brown. In many areas of Kent the use of ragstone (Kentish

(Facing page) 98. Ways of working stone walling according to the nature of stone: *clockwise from top left* – combined use of large and small stones; finely jointed random sized limestone; boulder stones set on thin courses of slate; banded limestone and flint; mixture of chalk and sand; slate; sandstone; mixture of assorted and various sized stones

rag) is characteristic. The sandstone around Horsham in West Sussex has also been widely used for roofing. The dominant material throughout the region is flint with brick, but along the shoreline in Sussex beach pebbles or cobbles have regularly been used instead of flint (Fig. 99).

99. Pebble walling, similar in appearance to flint

Wessex
(Avon, Dorset, Hampshire, Wiltshire, Berkshire and Oxfordshire)
There are extensive deposits of limestone in the area, the best known being the Portland, Bath and Purbeck stones. Portland stone is either greyish white or pale cream, whilst Purbeck is a distinctive blue grey, and has been much used in church work. Quarried by the Romans and the Saxons, Bath stone is ideal for carving detail and ornamentation and is one of the most widely used native stones. The mellow honey to yellow shades have a particular charm but it is vulnerable to pollution and is easily soiled. An example on how finely it can be worked is shown in Fig. 100, but many old buildings have become badly affected by the soiling problem. A cold grey limestone known as blue lias is much evident in west Dorset and extends into Somerset. In other parts of Dorset the limestone is a warm yellowish brown due to the presence of iron oxide in the soil.

100. Georgian house, Avon

Much of the fine limestone in Oxfordshire lies in the Cotswold belt (see below) but the stone from the nearby Headington Quarry is prevalent around the city of Oxford and weathers to a mild grey. In the north of the county, stone from the Horton Quarry has produced a blue-grey or brownish stone. The limestones in Wiltshire are more likely to be a mild grey. At the extreme western tip of Berkshire, Cotswold stone has been used, but elsewhere there is a predominance of flint and brick. Much of the stone in the Cotswolds has also been used for roofing. North of Newbury an extensive chalk stratum has resulted in a considerable amount of chalk blockwork, especially at Uffington and the surrounding areas.

The Cotswolds
(The southern part of Oxfordshire and the eastern side of Gloucestershire)
The limestone in this area is fine grained and a pleasing honey colour. It is also softer and easier to tool, which has resulted in more intricate detailing and decorative design work. On the western side of Gloucestershire near the Forest of Dean there is a rich stratum of pennant sandstone that varies in various shades of grey, brown and red.

The West Country
(Cornwall, Devon and Somerset)
The blue lias limestone that extends into Somerset differs little from that found in Dorset except that in parts it is harder and coarser and can be more difficult to work. Where this occurs a different stone has often been used at the quoins (corners) and door and window openings. Granite is the traditional material for Cornwall and comes in various shades of grey. Mostly a lighter grey, it is sometimes found speckled and can be seen as a light grey with a hint of fawn. A notable exception is the granite from Lantoom, which is mostly rustic but sometimes brown or grey.

In parts of Cornwall slatestone was also used for walling, the more notable variety being that quarried from Tredinnick, which is either red or fawn. Serpentine has also been used and is identifiable through a veined green appearance that can also be mottled. In the natural state serpentine is clearly visible at the Lizard headland. The fine-grained grey-green slate from Delabole is a feature of local roofing.

In addition to cob, sandstone was widely used in Devon, where it can have wide variations in colour. This can go from a greenish yellow, to red purple, brown and deep yellow. In the areas concerned, many of the vernacular buildings have been either rendered or whitewashed, obliterating the colour of the stone. In the area around Beer the hard shelly, cream-coloured Beerstone was the main building medium.

Nodules of light brown chert are a feature of the Chard area of Somerset and the Axminster district of Devon. A small outcrop of silver-grey granite around Yelverton in Devon has been used for walling around the area.

West Midlands
(Herefordshire and Worcestershire, Shropshire, Warwickshire, Staffordshire,
Cheshire and Derbyshire)
Shropshire has extensive deposits of a whiteish-grey sandstone that changes
to a yellowish grey in the more southern parts of the county. A sandstone
belt running through Hereford and Worcester changes considerably in
colour in places – from red, pink, purple, brown, grey green and different
shades of grey. Another series passing through Warwick, Worcestershire
and Staffordshire alters in colour from grey to grey with a tinge of green,
but in some parts this colour switches to a brownish red or purple.

Derbyshire is an important building stone area, with the local sandstone
being very close grained and durable. It varies in colour from pink, yellow,
grey, bluish and mauve and works well. It is mostly found squared and
uniform, often with precise ornamentation. In Staffordshire the colour
range is more limited and is either off-white or pink to red. In Cheshire
most of the sandstones are either a pink or a fawny grey.

Eastern Shires
(Nottinghamshire, Lincolnshire, Leicestershire, Northamptonshire,
Cambridgeshire, Buckinghamshire, Bedfordshire and parts of
Herefordshire)
The sandstones in Northamptonshire are predominantly cream or brown,
except for the stone quarried at Mansfield, which is a deep red. The
limestone quarry at Colley Weston produces the well-known roofing slate.
In Nottinghamshire the main sandstone streams are either red or white.

Much of the limestone in the county is either a shade of brown or is
rust coloured. In some parts the stone has a distinct hint of green. Towards
the southern boundary much of the stone quarried is a pale grey. The
contrasting colours within a relatively small area have been exploited to
good effect in some buildings which have two different coloured stones
in alternating bands. In Buckinghamshire and Bedfordshire most of the
local limestone is coarse and crumbles easily, which has resulted in a
large number of buildings being externally rendered. Conversely, the
limestone series extending from Leicestershire through to Lincolnshire
and Humberside is of a high quality. Lincolnshire limestone is highly
rated, especially stone from the Ancaster Quarry near Sleaford, which is
either creamy white, bluish or brown. The fine-grained stone from Ketton
is either cream or a pale pink.

East Anglia
(Norfolk, Suffolk and Essex)
In the north-west of Norfolk there is a small stratum of a rich golden brown sandstone known locally as carstone, otherwise the area is largely bereft of suitable building stone. In the north and east of Norfolk much use has been made of cobbles from the estuaries and seashore, and elsewhere flint is very prominent. In the Hunstanton area a hard chalk stratum has been used in a similar way to Cambridgeshire clunch (see below), with various hues of colourwash being used as a protective coating.

Lake District
(Cumbria and the northern tip of Lancashire)
Cobblestone, slatestone and sandstone are the dominant materials for the area. The slatestones used for walling have a special appeal and vary in colour. The slate in the Burlington district ranges from grey blue to purple or a light grey, whereas the Westmorland seam that extends into north Lancashire is grey green. Coniston slate is a different light green; it was much used broken into long strips in conjunction with cobblestone.

Cumbrian cobblestones vary considerably in colour, being lumps of rock that were washed into the valleys and lowlands through glacier action during the Ice Age. Rounded in form, they were also popular for working corners and door and window openings with other materials, including slate, and are used in some parts as alternating bands with slate. The sandstones of the Eden Vale tend to be a uniform pink or modest red but in the Penrith area the stone is an exceptionally bright red, giving the buildings a particular character.

In Cumbria granite from the Broad Oak Quarry near Waberthwaite has been used in a limited way for walling. It can be recognized from a blue-grey colour speckled with dark grey veining. Much of the slate quarried in Cumbria is used for roofing.

Northern Counties
(Northumberland, Durham, Cleveland, North, South and West Yorkshire, Tyne and Wear, Humberside and Lancashire)
The north of England has an abundance of good-quality building stones, with many of the finest being located in the Yorkshire area. Most of the deposits are sandstone, but in North Yorkshire there is a small seam of magnesian limestone. Most limestones contain small amounts of

carbonate of magnesia, and when in it appears in high quantities it is called magnesian limestone. If magnesium carbonate and calcium carbonate are present in equal quantities the stone is called dolomitic. One of the best-known limestones from the region is quarried at Huddleston and is a pale gold. Another much-used limestone comes from Hovingham and is either grey or creamy white in colour. Other local limestones are the pale fawn Silverdale and the light fawn Tadcaster.

Much of the sandstone for high-class work comes from the Bolton Wood Quarry and is a light brown. Bramley Fell millstone grit ranges from white to cream or yellow. Gritstones are strong, hard and durable, with the grains often being coarse and angular. A particularly robust millstone grit (so called because its texture is ideally suited for grinding corn: the grains of the stone are sharp and angular, whereas most other sandstones are smoother and more rounded) is quarried at Moorfield and is light brown. Greenmoor blue is a close-grained sandstone and is either blue, brown or gold. Dead Friars is a buff-coloured and medium-grained sandstone. The light buff Hard York sandstone is fine grained and highly suitable for working in detail. In Lancashire, Revidge grit is available in various shades of brown, grey and blue. The Appley Bridge blue stone has a particularly fine texture. In Tyne and Wear the Blaxter sandstone is cream, whereas Cat Castle sandstone in Durham is a distinctive white and streaky brown.

The Use of Flint

The Chalk Formations
In composition flint is a near-pure form of crypto-crystalline silica and, although it is virtually imperishable, it possesses some curious characteristics. It is hard and dense in structure but it is also brittle and can be easily fractured. It occurs in natural form as nodules in the upper and middle chalk formations of England but in some areas can sometimes be found at surface level as a result of long-term erosion of the chalk (Fig. 101). The main deposits are in the south-eastern and eastern regions, with the best examples used in building found in the counties of Suffolk, Norfolk, Sussex and Kent.

Flint should not be confused with chert, which, although similar, is never present in the chalk strata and is essentially a feature of some sedimentary rock formations. Chert is a siliceous microcrystalline substance found principally in the connecting border areas between Devon, Cornwall and

Somerset and in parts of Yorkshire. It has characteristics similar to flint but is usually much lighter in colour, with the nodules tending to be much larger.

Knapped and Gauged Work
Flint can be laid as found and in this form it is described as undressed and is set either coursed or uncoursed. It can also be knapped or knapped and gauged. Knapping is a method of fracturing flint nodules into two or more pieces to reveal a grey-black lustrous surface that is often flecked

When taken from the ground the nodules are covered with a white crust of lime. Minerals sometimes cause this to be tinted.

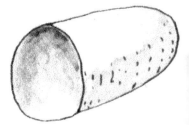

The knapped surfaces reveal an opaque material usually grey black or dark brown in colour.

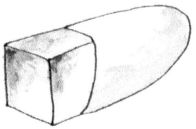

Knapped and squared flints are assembled to produce a bonding effect identical to brick or stone work.

101. Flint nodules

with white. Sometimes lighter grey and greyish blue colours result. The technique requires skill and is achieved by a short sharp blow with a tool; an antler would have been used for this purpose in times past.

Gauged work was a later progression whereby the knapped stones were also squared (Fig. 102). The use of knapped flint first appeared around AD 1200 and opened up new horizons in terms of aesthetics and wall texturing. From about 1760 onwards, knapped and gauged flintwork became very popular in certain classes of construction. A particular disadvantage in flint building is the difficulty in achieving an effective bond between the flints and the mortar and the weakness this caused at the quoins. Builders overcame this by using brick or stone at the quoins and gave added strength with the use of intermediate courses of the same material – described as lacing courses (Fig. 103).

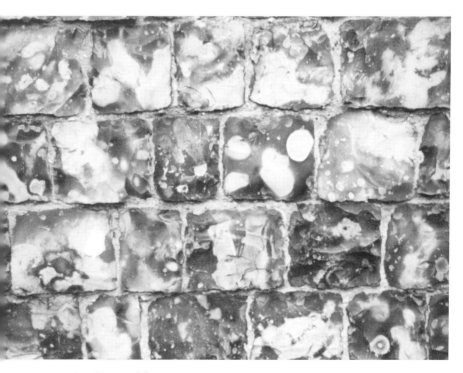

102. Knapped and squared flint

103. Flint-and-brick cottage, West Sussex

Chequer-work and Flushwork

At the beginning of the fourteenth century, flint worked in combination
with other materials resulted in the introduction of chequer-work (Fig. 104)
and in the fifteenth century the widespread appearance of a technique
known as flushwork became popular (Fig. 105). Indigenous to East Anglia,
the latter involves the cutting of hollows and cavities into ashlared stone
to receive an infilling of knapped and dressed flint bedded in mortar.
Chequer-work is the alternate use of squares of dressed stone and flint.
Both techniques are mostly seen on buildings of substance.

Medieval builders sometimes used a technique known as galleting (also
referred to as garneting or garreting), which involved inserting small slivers
of flint into the mortar jointing of the facework before it had set (Fig. 106).
The practice is recorded in a journal dated 1514, relating to work at the
Tower of London, but it is known to have been in use much earlier.

Tabular flints have a characteristic flat surface and are laid in a manner
similar to Kentish ragstone (Fig. 107). A considerable amount of tabular
work can be seen in the Chichester area of West Sussex. Gnarled flints are
the irregular shapes which cannot be utilized in the normal way but they
do have a decorative function. In parts of Devon flint was often used with
alternating bands of roughly dressed stone.

104. Chequer-work walling

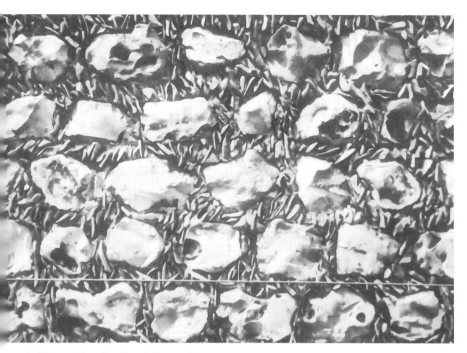

106. Knapped and galleted flintwork

107. Tabular flint intermixed with flint nodules

(*Facing page*) 105. Flushwork, East Anglia

CHALK AS A BUILDING MATERIAL

The Chalk Formations
In the past chalk has been widely used as a building material, especially where it was readily accessible and could be transported at reasonable cost. Moreover it offered considerable versatility in the manner in which it could be worked. The chalk formations are located mainly in the upland parts of southern England, but deposits can also be found in some lowland areas, particularly in Norfolk, Suffolk and Cambridgeshire. It is also present in parts of northern England, more notably in Lincolnshire and the East Riding of Yorkshire.

In the British Isles the chalk strata vary considerably in composition and quality, with the harder and more rock-like varieties often being described as clunch. This is a term that is often imprecise and should really be applied to a particular type of chalk found in Cambridgeshire and Bedfordshire. The chalk in this region has a higher calcite content and is harder and denser than in most other strata. It can be identified by a distinctive gritty texture due to the presence of silica. This, and chalk from other parts, was used in block form (Fig. 108), and many well-preserved examples can be found in ashlar, roughly dressed and random rubble work. It was often favoured as a complementary material in buildings constructed of flint, brick and certain types of stone. Where chalk block has been used in isolation there has been a tendency towards rendering walls at a later date, displacing an earlier practice of coating it with either a limewash or a chalk slurry. Most chalk stones are relatively soft and easier to work than other building stones and for this reason the material became popular for use in ashlar and ornamental work. At one stage it was much favoured for vaulting and internal decorative features in churches and cathedrals.

Impurities and Colour
Chalk is really a soft limestone derived from microscopic marine organisms, and in its purest form is 95 per cent calcium carbonate. Most chalks, however, contain impurities such as quartz, glauconite, iron pyrites and other minerals that produce a slight discolouration. This can vary from cream to pale grey, pale green or pink, and may sometimes be found in deeper tones. A well-known tinted chalk is Devon Beerstone.

108. Cottage with external facing in roughly dressed chalk blockwork

Chalk Cob and Chalk Mud Lump

Crushed chalk mixed with straw and clay was used in wet mass form in a similar fashion to unbaked earth. More usually described as chalk cob, the work progressed in lifts in a similar manner to clay cob but had the advantage of drying more speedily. Wychert, which is only found in parts of Buckinghamshire and Oxfordshire, is a natural blend of chalk and clay. An entirely different construction technique was used in parts of Wiltshire and Cambridgeshire and involved breaking down the chalk so that it could be formed into blocks. Known as chalk mud lump or pugged chalk, this entailed ramming moist chalk pug into moulds, in a similar way to clay lump. The blocks were then left to dry until ready for use and were bonded in a similar way to brickwork, using either a lime/sand mortar or a clay/sand slurry, often containing the addition of lime putty. A further variation was the pise method of construction, which used broken-down chalk placed almost dry. The chalk was rammed and compacted between shuttering, and the operation was carried out in lifts or layers.

COBBLES, PEBBLES AND BOULDERS

As already described, cobbles and pebbles were used for building along the coastal fringes of Sussex, a small part of Kent and certain locations along the shoreline of Norfolk and Suffolk (Fig. 99). Worn to rounded irregular shapes, the stones were taken from streams, estuaries and the seashore to be laid in a similar fashion to undressed flint. Stones over 3" (7 cm) and no more than 12" (30 cm) in diameter are termed cobbles, whilst those under 3" (7 cm) are called pebbles. Boulders are those over 12" (30 cm) in diameter and are frequently set with smaller stones, which are sometimes used as positioning wedges. Cyclopean stones are those of a gigantic size.

HISTORIC BRICKWORK

Early Brick Making

The firing of clay bricks has early origins, with the ancient Chinese being accredited as the discoverers of the process. It was later adopted by the Egyptians and then used extensively by the Romans, who introduced brick building to Britain. It remains a mystery why the process was abandoned after their departure and did not re-emerge for nearly a thousand years.

During their occupation the Romans raised building standards to high levels, but they never acquired the ability to fire clays to high temperatures. This was overcome by moulding bricks into thin slabs, which enabled sufficient heat to be generated for fusion to take place. In appearance Roman bricks are more like thick tiles and are recorded in Latin as *tegulae*, which means tile (Fig. 109). A derivative of this description continued with the early English bricks being described as *waltyles* (wall tiles), with references to brick not appearing in the building vocabulary until the beginning of the fifteenth century. Roman bricks are often found in later construction owing to a practice in medieval times of reclaiming them for use with other materials.

109. Roman brickwork

The First English Bricks

The first English bricks were made around the year 1200 but, due to cost, were not used at vernacular level until well into the seventeenth century (Fig. 110). Brick building began in those parts of the country where superficial deposits of clay were readily extractable and close at hand. At first the clay was usually fired on site in rudimentary clamps. The best quality bricks came from the centre of the clamp; many of the outer bricks were left soft and under-burnt. Known as sammel bricks, these substandard blocks were picked out and used for rough work and are usually pinkish in colour.

There were no standard sizes – some bricks were cumbersome and difficult to handle. Sizes could vary from 15" to 20" (38–50 cm) in length and 6" to 11" (15–28 cm) in width. Known as 'great bricks', these had to

be laid on thick beds of lime/sand mortar due to the irregularities in their shape and texture. The influx of skilled Flemish labour into East Anglia in the late thirteenth century provided the impetus for an improvement in standards and the quality of work. The Flemings had considerably more experience of the trade, and introduced smaller bricks with a better texture designed to fit the hand for easier working. Lengths varied from 6¼" to 8¼" (16–21 cm) by about 3¼" (8 cm) in width and 1½" to 1¾" (3–4.5 cm) in thickness. The Flemish influence also had an effect on style, with ornamental Dutch gables appearing in the east coast port areas extending from Kent to Humberside and more especially in East Anglia (Fig. 111).

110. Early medieval brickwork

111. Stansted Hall, Essex. The Dutch gables are a characteristic feature of the area.

The Improvement in Standards

The haphazard manner in which bricks had been laid in early medieval times was superseded at the beginning of the Tudor period by the use of alternating headers and stretchers (a header is a brick displaying the small end face; a stretcher is a brick displaying the long side face), later to become known as English bond (Fig. 112). It heralded the start of a great age for brick

and resulted in the introduction of intricate shapes and sizes that competed with stone detailing in attractiveness. Skilled tradesmen took brick building to new peaks by creating distinctive features in moulded brick such as twisted chimney stacks, turrets, pinnacles, delicate arches and spires (Fig. 113). Other innovations produced diaper patterning and the use of over-burnt bricks to form darker diamond-shaped grids. Most bricks of the period have a distinctive colour and a coarse texture with irregular surfaces and slight distortions in shape (Fig. 114). At this stage, dimensions became more uniform,

112. English bond

113. Chimney with moulded bricks

114. Tudor brickwork

115. Flemish bond

with most bricks measuring 9½ x 4⅜ x 2" (24 x 11 x 5 cm). From Tudor times until the early seventeenth century English bond remained in use, but a change in fashion caused a switch to Flemish bond until a revival of English bond in the nineteenth century (Fig. 115). Flemish bond used alternating stretchers and headers in each course of brickwork. Although taken to highly sophisticated levels, brick was seldom used for church building until Victorian times.

Gauged Brickwork and Tuck Pointing
Carefully worked dressings required different techniques, and gauged brickwork answered this need. Soft-textured bricks were roughly sawn to size and then rubbed to a smooth surface, giving precise dimensions (Fig. 116). A growing demand for lighter bricks led to the introduction

116. Gauged brickwork to window heads. Fine lime mortar is used to assemble the sawn and rubbed bricks. This form of brickwork was popular in the late seventeenth century until well into the eighteenth century.

of the indentation known as the frog, a term taken from the old English word *frogga*, meaning a hollow. The Georgian period is regarded as having produced some of the finest brickwork and was also the time of tuck pointing, a technique that remained in use until the early nineteenth century (Fig. 117). Tuck pointing was used to mimic the appearance of gauging by placing rough bricks in mortar that was the same colour as the bricks. Fine recesses were cut into the partially dry mortar, which were then pointed in lime mortar to give the impression of gauged brickwork. Contrary to popular belief, brick size is not a positive guide to age; a more reliable approach is to examine the character and texture of the material, and the manner in which it has been laid and bonded.

Local Variations

Before mass production, the colour and quality of bricks differed between regions and even between locations of close proximity. The final product was highly dependent on good husbandry and the constituent nature of

117. Tuck pointing

the clay. The presence and amount of impurities and metallic oxides was a determining factor in the quality and colour of the finished product.

The clay deposits in Durham, Hampshire, Lancashire, Leicester, Yorkshire and deposits near Peterborough produced good bricks in varying shades of red. The depth of the colour was reliant on the amount of red oxide present.

The calcareous clays in Cambridgeshire, Lincolnshire and Suffolk have a low iron oxide content that, when kilned, produce the well-known 'white' bricks, which in reality are usually a pale cream. The gault clays that encircle the Kentish and Sussex Weald also result in pale yellow bricks. Local bricks in the Fenlands are more likely to be found buff coloured. The clay strata running through Berkshire and Buckinghamshire were able to produce high-quality bricks in various shades of red, grey and blue, and a very high standard of brickwork can be found in these areas. The various colours were regularly used in combination to create artistic features in polychrome (Fig. 118).

The clays running through the Chilterns gave brown-red bricks and a similar clay in the Bedfordshire and Huntingdon areas resulted in brindled bricks. A few of the clays in the midland regions produced subdued red-brown bricks, but most were a bright red – especially the famous 'Accrington bloods', which had a high colour intensity . Elsewhere in the region the bricks were lighter in colour but nevertheless still a strong red.   In the Trent Valley the clays always produced very dark brown bricks that were at times almost black. No hard-and-fast rules or clear guidance can be given to identifying locally made bricks, and the scene rapidly became confused and blurred when improved means of transport enabled bricks to be carted long distances at reasonable cost. By the seventeenth century, many of the gentry houses were being built of brick with stone dressings, typical examples being Stansted House near Rowlands Castle in Hampshire (Fig. 119) and the National Trust property Uppark, not far from Chichester (Fig. 120).

118. Polychrome brickwork

119. Stansted House, Rowlands Castle, Hampshire. The original house was built
in 1688 and has since been substantially altered and enlarged.

120. Uppark, West Sussex. Built around 1690, the house was badly damaged by fire in 1989 and has since been carefully restored.

Roof Coverings

The natural harmony that local roof materials share with their immediate surroundings imparts a special quality to the buildings they protect. There was seldom a choice of materials, and utilization was largely dictated by availability, economics and climatic influences.

Thatch

The most extensively used material until the end of the medieval period was thatch, and in rural areas this preference continued well into the nineteenth century, the exception being those regions that had plentiful supplies of either slate or stone. The craft of thatching is one of the most ancient building skills and existed where settlements had an adequate supply of water and plenty of fertile land, which offered perfect conditions for producing bountiful crops of straw. In areas lacking in such good fortune, people used alternative materials such as heather (known as ling), turf, fern, bracken, flax and sedge. In some districts sedge was used exclusively for capping ridges.

Most of the roofing straws came from wheat, oats, rye or barley, with wheat being the most widely used in southern England. It was laid by the long-straw method. In reality long-straw thatching is no longer than any other wheat straw, and has acquired the name from the method of application, which allows a considerable length of straw to be visible on the surface of the roof. The alternative is combed straw, which is also known as Devon reed. The difference is in the way the wheat straw has been placed and combed out and this technique can be recognized by the exposed butt ends of the stalks on the outer surface. Around the Norfolk Broads reed was grown exclusively for thatching, being tougher and more durable than all the other materials. Reed was also used in a limited way in other areas where it could be grown in wetlands, the more notable places being parts of Dorset and Hampshire. In exposed locations thatch had to be lashed down with rope made of twisted straw (or sometimes bracken stems) to prevent wind damage, with projecting stone pegs being built into the walls as fixing points (Fig. 121). The majority of these roofs have since been replaced with either slate or tile with the projecting stone pegs remaining as a reminder of the past.

121. Thatched roofing held secure by a network of ropes fastened at the gable ends

Plain Tiling

Throughout the Middle Ages shingles (wood tiles) were widely used, but a trend started in the more prestigious buildings towards clay tiling, and the fashion gradually expanded down the social scale to the smaller dwellings and farm buildings. Although clay tiling came a long time before brick, it did not evolve into a recognizable industry until the thirteenth century. Once established, it rapidly grew in favour in the Weald, Wessex and the southern parts of both the west midlands and the eastern shires. The early plain tiles were made with two holes at the head for fixing with wooden pegs, but sometimes they can be found secured with sheep knuckle bones in lieu of pegs. In the eighteenth century, knibs started to replace peg holes, reviving a practice that originated in Roman times (knibs are small clay projections on the underface of a tile that prevent the tile from slipping from the fixing batten). This form of tiling also became popular as a wall cladding at first-floor level (Fig. 122).

122. Tile-hanging to first-floor elevation

Pantiling

Single lap tiling (pantiling) has a different history and first appeared in the eastern counties of England towards the end of the seventeenth century as a direct result of trade links with Holland. This influence also made a localized impact around the Bridgewater area of Somerset for the same reason. After a period of importation, local production began and became an important industry. In general terms the early products were not precisely made and needed to be fixed with moss and torching to make them weather resistant (torching is lime mortar mixed with animal hair applied to the underside of a slate or tile as a means of achieving a better fix). Eventually pantiling extended into other parts of the country, reaching as far as Yorkshire (excluding the Dales), together with large areas of the eastern half of the northern counties. It is difficult to form a satisfactory verge with pantiles, which is the reason why they are more regularly used with parapets at the gable ends.

Slate and Stone Roofing

The contrasts at vernacular level are never more apparent than in the districts where natural slate or stone have been used for roofing. The main zones of this are to be found in the Lake District, Cornwall, parts of Devon and Leicestershire. The climate and local circumstances dictated variations in working methods that are significant and involved the use of natural slate, limestone and sandstone.

SLATE

The grey Delabole slates in Cornwall were often used in random sizes, and in severely exposed areas are regularly found bedded in lime mortar. Sometimes they were coated with a cement slurry, or dressed with red lead or tar to help counter the ravages of the Atlantic storms. A highly individualistic style developed in the Lake District, where the attractive green-coloured slates were rounded at the heads, with a single fixing hole and peg, and were laid in courses of diminishing sizes ranging from 24" (61 cm) at the eaves to 6" (15 cm) at the ridge. In the same region Wrestler slates are used, so called because they are dressed to interlock to prevent uplift and slippage from wind pressure and other movements. The natural slate in Devon is more often grey or grey green and sometimes has traces of rust. The slates in Leicestershire are a blue grey.

LIMESTONE

In locations where limestone has been used the application depended on how it could be split and trimmed. The result is an interesting variation in styles throughout the country and coverings are classified into either stone slates (sometimes referred to as tiles) or flags, which are much heavier and larger in size. To be suited to this type of use the stone had to be naturally fissile. The pale cream to light yellow limestones in the Cotswolds were trimmed into various tile sizes and given quaint sounding names such as wivetts, muffties, tants and cussems, which all have a meaning. The limestone strata elsewhere have produced a wide variety of styles including such well known names such as Colleyweston slates from Northamptonshire, which are bedded on slightly recessed ribbons or pats of lime mortar and have cream to grey colouration. Purbeck limestone has also been widely used for roofing and varies in hue from grey to blue grey.

SANDSTONE

Sandstones slates and tiles are generally much thicker and heavier, which tends to place limitations on roof configuration. As a result, most sandstone roofs are more simplistic and to a lower pitch. A large number of tiles were produced in the sandstone belt around Horsham in West Sussex and in the Pennines. The production of sandstone tiles or flags also covered Derbyshire, Staffordshire, east Lancashire and Shropshire, through to West Yorkshire. In Derbyshire the slates are fixed with one peg with a rounded head and are mostly slate grey in colour, but some outcrops produce yellow or yellowy pink slates. In Cheshire slates from the Kerridge Quarry are shades of fawn to grey. Some districts had local preferences in fixing, with stone slates at the eaves and other materials being used higher up the slope. Every ancient technique represents inventiveness and creativity. Through these attributes the craftsmen of the time created a host of fascinating and highly pleasing features that make a unique contribution to the richness of the English landscape.

THE EFFECT OF SOCIAL CHANGE

The modern tendency towards using products to replicate another material is not new. As architectural tastes and social attitudes altered, it became fashionable to give buildings from an earlier period a facelift. This occurred widely during the eighteen century, when many medieval and Elizabethan mansions underwent dramatic alterations to the Palladian style. Much of the Classical detail and imitation ashlar was undertaken in stucco, with natural stone being restricted mostly to buildings of particular importance.

Changes in living patterns also resulted in major alterations internally. The house in Fig. 123 is now substantially different from when it was built. As a medieval manor house it originally had an open central hall with cross-wings at either end. Now altered to a modern design, the up-to-date windows and a large lean-to entrance porch conceal substantial parts of the original structure.

123. Converted medieval manor house

11 Vernacular Styles – Some Notable Features

The vernacular buildings of England are the product of ingenuity, skill and perseverance by the people who constructed them using locally available materials to the best effect. The legacy they left tells us much about the needs and priorities of the time and the difficulties the various communities overcame. As already described, visual impressions may not always convey an accurate picture; as tastes altered, elevations were reconstructed using materials such as brick cladding, mathematical tiles or worked stucco. Houses that give the appearance of having been built in stone or brick may in fact be wholly timber-framed with an outer cladding added at a later date. Also it was sometimes the practice to fill in the jettied overhang in either brick or stone to make additional space in the ground-floor rooms.

Local materials and fashions were generally the dominant factors that determined style and appearance. The following are some characteristic types. Fig. 125 overleaf shows the county boundaries of England.

~

~ The soft and easily worked nature of the limestone in the Cotswolds made it possible for architectural details of high quality and refinement to be worked, which can occur even in the most lowly of buildings. Dormers (so called because the space was used

124. Limestone Cotswold farmhouse

125. Map of county boundaries of England

for sleeping) in the front elevation are a particular feature of the area (Fig. 124). Other characteristics are the long stone head and mullioned windows and the stone slate roof coverings.

~ In Kent and the neighbouring counties the external clapboarding used in the cottages and small houses mostly dates from the eighteenth century.

~ In Somerset, cottages and small houses generally have windows in thick heavy stonework; many have the front door in the gable end and the chimney stack in the same gable. Most buildings in this style date from the seventeenth century.

~ From the late sixteenth century onwards brick and stud construction with a hipped roof became popular in the south-east, often with tile-hanging to the first-floor level. It was chosen as a way to reduce the impact of the brick tax.

~ In East Anglia the brick and flint cottages of the area are often found with a centrally placed front door, with windows either side and small dormer windows immediately above. The steepness of the roof pitch regularly made it impracticable to extend the roof at the rear to create an outshot. As a result, extensions are regularly found attached to a gable wall.

~ In Cornwall the original fishermen's cottages share similarities with the bastle houses in the border areas of northern England, with the living accommodation at first-floor level and the space underneath reserved for storage. A traditional Cornish granite-built cottage is depicted in Fig. 126, and it was the practice there to cover the roof slates with a cement slurry to help prevent them from being dislodged by gale-force winds coming in from the Atlantic.

126. Cottage in Cornwall built in local granite with a stone slate roof

~ An interesting feature of the Lake District and surrounding areas is the 'watershot' technique used in the walling, whereby the stones are set at an outward slope to dispel penetrating rain. The round corbelled chimney stacks are another characteristic (Fig. 127), with the roofs being covered with Cumbrian slate laid in courses that diminish in size towards the ridge. The use of slate window sills together with undressed slate lintels is also customary in the area.

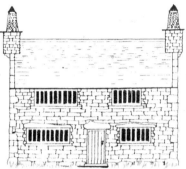

127. Lake District farmhouse

~ Some very meagre cottages can also be found on the Yorkshire Moors. Built of local stone they normally have one room on the ground floor and a single bedroom overhead, with each room having a centrally placed window, and the front access door set to one side. West Yorkshire is the homeland for a particular style of millstone grit cottages that can also be found in some areas of north and south Yorkshire and in parts of Lancashire. The cottages are built in large millstone grit blocks with sandstone subframes around the windows, and the copings to the parapets at the gable ends are supported by distinctive projecting kneelers (Fig. 128). A notable characteristic is the use of pale mortar, which is in marked contrast to the dark millstone grit blocks.

128. West Yorkshire millstone grit cottage

~ Early Devon farmhouses regularly have a side chimney with an unusual termination, which can also be seen around the neighbouring border areas of Wiltshire. This chimney includes an adjoining bread oven visible externally as a bulbous projection (Fig. 129).

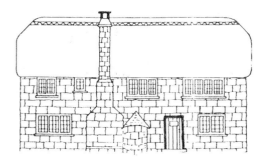

129. Devon farmhouse

~ In mid-Kent, the southern part of Surrey and some areas of the Sussex downland, ironstone provided a local alternative to timber or flint. The very dark forms are sometimes described as carstone and were used as rubblework (Fig. 130).

130. Wealden cottage of brick and ironstone

~ In locations where outcrops occur in the west midlands, large new red sandstone blocks have been used extensively (the term is applied to sandstones from the Triassic and Old Permian series). They were often cut to expansive sizes and relate to the way the stone could be lifted from thick natural stratifications (Fig. 131). Unfortunately, this makes them out of proportion when used in the small vernacular buildings and gives an unsuitable focus.

131. West Midlands sandstone cottage

~ The differences between the regions is especially emphasized by the longhouse, which is never found in the south-east of England but is a particular feature in north-east Yorkshire, parts of Cumbria and much of the south-west. Towards the end of the eighteenth century, builders started to show an interest in the mansard roof, which gave much-needed extra headroom in cottage designs, but the fashion did not persist and by the start of the Victorian period it had been completely abandoned.

~

As the transportation of materials became easier the vernacular styles started to decline in favour of more standardized cottage and small house designs. During the Renaissance an adaptation of the Italianate villa also appeared in the English countryside, the term later being misapplied by developers to describe a particular type of town house. By around the middle part of the nineteenth century a large number of rural workers were being housed in small semi-detached houses that were two rooms in depth. Most had a single-storey addition at the rear with an outshot roof that housed a copper, a coal store and an earth closet.

Appendices

The Appendices contain different lists, the selections having been chosen by the author as suitable places to visit, but the lists are not presented as being complete, definitive or fully comprehensive. This and the Tourist Offices Directory is given in good faith but circumstances can change, sometimes at short notice. No guarantee can therefore be made concerning the accuracy, completeness, availability or accessibility of any of the places or offices mentioned. Visitors need to check either directly with the places they intend to call on, or through a tourist information office before embarking on a journey to any of the places mentioned. Travelling by road to some of the locations listed can alter unexpectedly through roadworks, restrictions, accidents, highway rearrangements and other reasons, and checks need to be made with one of the approved motoring organizations before undertaking a journey to avoid possible delays, frustrations or extended travelling. The author and publishers accept no responsibility for any injury, loss, claim or damage arising out of the use or application of the book. Therefore, the information here should be used to indicate what is available.

~ APPENDIX A ~
# MUSEUMS WITH ITEMS OF INTEREST ON HISTORICAL BUILDINGS, INCLUDING HOW THEY WERE USED

BERKSHIRE
Museum of English Rural Life, Whiteknights, Reading
   On the Reading University Campus at Whiteknights, Reading.
   Open all year from Tuesday to Saturday.

CAMBRIDGESHIRE
Wimpole Farm, Near Cambridge (National Trust)
   The Farm is off the A14 about 8 miles south-west of Cambridge.
   Open daily March to October except Monday and Friday.

CORNWALL
Chysauster Ancient Village, Near Penzance (English Heritage)
   An interesting settlement dating back to the Iron Age. Each house is a series of
      circular stone rooms.
   Off the B3311 about 4 to 5 miles north of Penzance.
   Open all year daily.

CUMBRIA
Museum of Lakeland Life and Industry, Abbot Hall, Kendal
   Close to junction 37 on the M6. From the junction take the A684 to Kendal.
   Open 10.30 am to 4 pm April to October. Closed Sunday.

DURHAM
North of England Open-Air Museum, Beamish Hall, Stanley, Durham
   Stanley is on the A693 near Derwent Park and is about 4 miles west of
      Chester-le-Street.
   Open daily but not on Mondays between November and March.

GLOUCESTERSHIRE
Gloucester Folk Museum, Westgate Street, Gloucester
   From the M5 junction 11A take the main road to Gloucester.
   Open all year Tuesday to Sunday 10 am to 5 pm.

HAMPSHIRE

Pimperne Open-Air Exhibition, Queen Elizabeth Park, near Petersfield

The buildings have been re-created from evidence found on an Iron Age site in Dorset.

On the A3 between Petersfield and Havant. The site is about 4 miles south of Petersfield.

Open March to October daily. November to February Sundays only.

KENT

Museum of Kent Rural Life, Near Maidstone

The Museum is just off the A229 and is about 2 miles north of Maidstone.

Open April to October, Monday, Tuesday, Thursday and Friday. Also Saturday and Sunday pm only.

LINCOLNSHIRE

Museum of Lincolnshire Life, The Old Barracks, Burton Road, Lincoln

Travel to Newark-on-Trent on the A1 and take the A46 to Lincoln.

Open daily May to October 10 am to 5 pm.

NORTH YORKSHIRE

Ryedale Folk Museum, Hutton-Le-Hole

Take the A170 between Helmsley and Pickering and at Keldholme follow the signs to Hutton-le-Hole.

Open daily all year from 10 am to 5.30 pm (last admissions 4.30 pm).

OXFORDSHIRE

Great Coxwell Barn, Near Faringdon (National Trust)

The barn dates from the thirteenth century and has an interesting structure and is well preserved.

The site is about 1½ to 2 miles south of Faringdon.

Open daily all year.

SOMERSET

Somerset Rural Life Museum, Chilkwell Street, Glastonbury

Open April to October Tuesday to Friday 10 am to 5 pm. Saturday and Sunday 2 pm to 6 pm.

SUFFOLK

West Stow Anglo-Saxon Village, Near Bury St Edmunds
A village reconstructed from the remains of the original buildings. The
workmen used tools identical to those used by the original builders.
Off the A1101 on the section between Midenhall and Bury St Edmunds. The
village is about 5 miles north-west of Bury St Edmonds.
Open April to October pm daily except Monday.

Museum of East Anglian Life, Illiffe Way, Stowmarket
An open-air museum placed in around seventy acres of land with many
interesting features relating to life in the past.
Take the A45 running between Bury St Edmunds and Ipswich and at
Stowmarket follow the signs.
Open March to October.

SURREY

Rural Life Centre, Old Kiln Museum, Reeds Road, Tilford, Farnham
From the A31 from Farnham take the B3001 to Milford; turn off near Waverley
Abbey and follow the signs to Tilford.
Ring for opening times (phone: 01252 795571).

WORCESTERSHIRE

Avoncroft Museum of Buildings, Near Bromsgrove
The site is off the A38 about 2 miles south of Bromsgrove.
Open daily from June to August. Restricted opening thereafter.

WEST SUSSEX

Weald and Downland Open-Air Museum, Singleton, Near Chichester
Singleton is on the A286 between Chichester and Midhurst. The site is close
to Goodwood Race Course and The Trundle, which is a well-known
hillfort.
Open daily April to October. November to March Wednesday, Sunday and
most Bank Holidays.

WEST YORKSHIRE

Ryburn Farm Museum, Near Halifax
The site is on the B6113 about 5 miles west of Halifax.
Open daily from March to October, but Saturday, Sunday and Bank Holidays
pm only.

~ APPENDIX B ~
LIME KILNS TO VISIT

CORNWALL

Cotehele Quay, St Dominick, Saltash

See also Cotehele House in Appendix H part B.

Saltash is about 2 miles west of Plymouth. Take the A388 to Callington; follow the route to St Dominicks and then follow the minor road to Cotehele Quay.

Local tourist office will advise on viewing.

DEVON

Hartland Quay Museum, Bideford

Take the A39 running between Bideford and Stratton; at Dyke follow the B3248 to Hartland and then the minor road to Hartland Quay.

Local tourist office will advise on viewing.

NORTHUMBERLAND

Beadnell Kiln, Beadnell Harbour, Beadnell (National Trust)

Contact the National Trust for viewing times.

Holy Island Kiln

The island is approached by a causeway at low tide; Lindisfarne Castle and the Priory can also be viewed there.

The island is about 18 miles south of Berwick-on-Tweed; using the A1 take the Holy Island turning.

Tide tables are displayed at the entrance and times can be checked by ringing 01289 330733.

WEST MIDLANDS

Black Country Living Museum, Dudley

The large number of lime kilns near the Dudley Canal basin are a feature of the Black Country village.

On the A4037, about 3 miles from the M5 junction 2, about 1 mile north of Dudley.

Open daily March to December. January to February Wednesday to Sunday.

WEST SUSSEX

Amberley Museum, Amberley

Off the B2139 about 5 miles north of Arundel. The museum is close to Amberley railway station.

Open April to October Wednesday to Sunday and Bank Holiday Monday.

~ APPENDIX C ~
ABBEYS AND PRIORIES TO VISIT

BEDFORDSHIRE

Esltow Abbey, Near Bedford

Founded in 1075, part of the original nunnery has survived as the parish church. Nearby is a large campanile (a free-standing belltower) that dates from the fifteenth century.

About 1 to 1½ miles south of Bedford, close to the A6.

Open daily all year.

CAMBRIDGESHIRE

Denny Abbey, Cambridge (English Heritage)

The Benedictine Order came to the site in 1159, but little of the original remains. One surviving building has been restored and houses the Farmland Museum of Agricultural History. Just north of the museum, part of the early fourteenth-century structure has become a barn.

Some 6 to 7 miles north of Cambridge on the A10.

Open daily from April to October pm only.

CUMBRIA

Furness Abbey, Near Barrow-in-Furness (English Heritage)

Now a ruin, the monastery was founded in 1147. The remaining walls are impressive, and a number of interesting features have survived.

The site can be reached from a minor road just off the A590 about 5 to 6 miles north of Barrow-in-Furness.

Open all year daily.

DURHAM

Finchale Priory, Near Winchcombe, Durham (English Heritage)

This is on a riverside site that has monastic connections going back to 1196. The building is now a ruin.

The priory is on a minor road just off the A167 about 3½ miles north-east of Durham.

The site is open to the public between April and September, but check with the local tourist office for times.

GLOUCESTERSHIRE

Hailes Abbey, (National Trust and English Heritage)

A well-cared-for ruin.

The site is around 2 to 3 miles north-east of Winchcombe just off the B4632.

Open daily from April to October.

HAMPSHIRE

Netley Abbey, Netley, Near Southampton (English Heritage)

Built in 1239, some interesting features of the original building are still to be seen.

The site is about 4 miles east of Southampton, facing Southampton Water.

Normally free access during daylight hours.

NORFOLK

Creake Abbey, Near Fakenham (English Heritage)

The abbey was founded as a priory in 1189 and was elevated to abbey status in 1231.

Some 8 to 9 miles north-west of Fakenham. About 1 mile north of North Creake take the B1355.

Open all year daily.

NORTH YORKSHIRE

Fountains Abbey, Near Ripon, (National Trust and English Heritage)

Founded in 1132, this substantial ruin is now a World Heritage Site.

The site is about 4 miles west of Ripon and is accessed via a small road leading from the B6265.

Open daily except on Fridays during November, December and January. Also closed over the Christmas and New Year holiday period.

NORTHUMBRIA

Lindisfarne Priory, Holy Island

The priory is the centre from which Christianity was reintroduced to northern England in the seventh century. The ruins are open to the public. Lindisfarne Castle and Holy Island Kiln are nearby (see Appendices B and E).

Holy Island is approached by a causeway at low tide. The tide times are displayed at the entrance and can be checked by ringing 01289 330733.

Access is governed by the tides; phone 01289 389244 to arrange a viewing.

OXFORDSHIRE

Hurley Priory, Near Henley-on-Thames

The priory was built in 1086 and part survives as the parish church. Located close to the site is a medieval dovecot and a tithe barn.

About 3 to 4 miles east of Henley on the A427 road running between Marlow and Henley.

SOMERSET

Cleeve Abbey, Near Minehead (English Heritage)
A thirteenth-century monastery, some of which survives. The refectory dates from the fifteenth century. There is also an interesting gatehouse.
Off the A39 not far from the village of Watchet and about 5 to 6 miles south-east of Minehead.
Open all year daily.

Woodspring Priory, Near Weston-Super-Mare (National Trust)
The priory was founded around 1210, but after the dissolution became derelict. It was acquired by the National Trust in 1968 and then restored by the Landmark Trust.
Off the A370 about 4 miles north of Weston-Super-Mare.
Open daily all year.

~ APPENDIX D ~
MINING MUSEUMS TO VISIT

CORNWALL

Cambourne School of Mines, Geological Museum, Cambourne
Off the A30 between Cambourne and Hayle.
Normally open daily.

Geevor Tin Mine, Boscaswell, Pendeen
An early tin mine that continued in operation until 1990. Underground conducted tours are available and there is an interesting mining museum attached.
Take the B3306 between St Ives and St Just. At Pendeen follow the Boscaswell or museum signs.
Open Easter to October – times can be checked by phoning 01736 788662.

Poldark Mine, Near Helston
A tin mine that has been worked since Roman times. There are underground museum chambers that vividly portray mining life and ways in the past.
On the B3297 about 3 to 3½ miles north of Helston.
Open daily April to October.

DURHAM

Killhope Wheel Lead Mining Museum, Killhope
   The original mine and buildings have been restored.
   Off the A689 on the section between Alston and Stanhope, about 10 miles
      west of Stanhope.
   Open Easter to October daily.

NORTH YORKSHIRE

Tom Leonard Mining Museum, Skinningrove, Deepdale
   An ironstone museum that has access to an array of draft mines.
   Open April to October; check opening times.

NOTTINGHAMSHIRE

National Mining Museum, Near Retford
   Off the A1 about 5 miles east of Retford.
   Open daily all year except Monday.

SOUTH YORKSHIRE

Abbeydale Complex, Abbeydale Road South, Sheffield
   This is a working complex exhibiting the process of furnacing and the
      processing and making of iron and steel artefacts.
   Open April to October Monday to Thursday and Sunday.

STAFFORDSHIRE

Chatterley Whitfield Mining Museum, Tunstall, Stoke-on-Trent
   Off the A527 on the section between Newcastle-under-Lyme and Congleton.
      The Museum is about 1½ to 2 miles north-east of Tunstall.
   Open daily all year.

~ APPENDIX E ~
CASTLES TO VISIT

CHESHIRE

Beeston Castle, Near Chester (English Heritage)
   About 11 miles south of Chester, just off the A49. Very near the Little
      Budworth Country Park and close to the Cheshire Candle Workshops.
   Open daily all year.

CORNWALL

Pendennis Castle, Pendennis Point (English Heritage)
> Henry VIII built the early part of the castle, which was subsequently enlarged and strengthened by Elizabeth I as a guard against the Spanish Armada.
> About 1 to 1½ miles south-east of Falmouth.
> Open daily all year.

Restormel Castle, Near Lostwithiel (English Heritage)
> This is a good example of a shell keep. The remains include a gatehouse and the great hall.
> Just off the A390 about 1½ miles north of Lostwithiel.
> Open daily all year.

Tintagel Castle, Tintagel (English Heritage)
> The castle ruins are closely linked with local folklore and legend.
> About 5 to 6 miles north of Camelford. Take the A39 between Camelford and Bude and branch off on to the B3263.
> Open daily all year.

CUMBRIA

Munster Castle, Near Ravenglass
> The castle has a fine thirteenth-century Pele tower.
> Just off the A595 about ½ mile south of Ravenglass, which is close to the Sellafield Exhibition Centre.
> Open daily pm from Good Friday to September except Monday and every Bank Holiday Monday.

DEVON

Compton Castle, Near Torquay (National Trust)
> The castle was built around 1329. The main features are the portcullis entrances and the intersecting solar.
> Off the A381 along a narrow access road about 4 miles west of Torquay.
> Open April to October, Monday, Wednesday and Thursday.

DORSET

Corfe Castle, Isle of Purbeck (National Trust)
> The ruins stand on a high mound and date from the twelfth century. Some very important historical events are linked to the castle.
> On the A351 about 4 to 5 miles south-east of Wareham.
> Open daily March to October; November to February, Saturday and Sunday pm only.

EAST SUSSEX

Bodium Castle, Near Great Dixter (National Trust)
> A storybook vision of a castle. Built in 1385, it has a moat and large cylindrical
> towers to the east and west walls. The north front has a large gatehouse.
> Off the A229, which runs between Hastings and the A268.
> Open April to October. November to March daily except Sunday.

Herstmonceux Castle, Near Hailsham
> The castle dates from the fifteenth century and for many years has been the
> headquarters of the Royal Greenwich Observatory. It is built of brick with
> stone dressings. This is a most unusual building medium for the period.
> Just off the road running between Hailsham and Battle, 5 miles east of
> Hailsham.

ESSEX

Hadleigh Castle, Benfleet (English Heritage)
> A special feature is the Norman tower, which has a labyrinth of chambers and
> passages.
> Off the A13 roughly 5 miles west of Southend.
> Open daily all year.

Hedingham Castle, Hedingham.
> The castle dates from 1140. The Norman keep has changed little over the
> centuries. Special features of note are the banqueting hall, the minstrels'
> gallery and the gatehouse area.
> On the B1058 between Hedington and Sudbury.
> Open Easter and then May to October daily.

Mountfitchet Castle, Near Bishop's Stortford
> The original earth-and-timber castle was destroyed in earlier times but has
> now been recreated as an exact replica and includes weaponry, a siege
> engine and other features.
> Off the B1051 about 2 miles north of Bishop's Stortford.
> Open daily from mid-March to November.

Tilbury Fort, Tilbury
> A seventeenth-century military fort that has a series of protective moats.
> Off the A126 about ½ mile east of Tilbury.
> Open daily all year.

GLOUCESTERSHIRE

Berkeley Castle, Berkeley

The building has been well preserved and in 1327 King Edward II was held prisoner in the dungeon. During the Civil War the castle was captured by the Roundheads, who forced entry by making a large breach in the keep which is still visible.

Access is a turning from the B4059 which is just off the A38 close to Slimbridge Wildfowl Trust. The castle is around 12 to 13 miles south-west of Gloucester.

Open daily April to September but not Monday or Bank Holidays.

Sudeley Castle, Winchcombe

Much of the castle was destroyed by Cromwell during the Civil War. Most of the working part is a nineteenth-century restoration and contains a number of interesting exhibits. The chapel contains the tomb of Catherine Parr, the sixth wife of Henry VIII.

Turn off the B4632 at Winchcombe onto the minor road connecting the B4632 with the A436. The castle is about 5 to 6 miles north-east of Cheltenham.

Open daily April to October.

KENT

Dover Castle, Dover (English Heritage)

Since the twelfth century the castle has guarded the English Channel at its narrowest point. Many interesting features can be seen.

Just north of Dover, overlooking the town. The best access is from Castle Hill Road.

Open daily all year.

Hever Castle, Near Edenbridge

The castle is where Ann Boleyn spent her childhood and has a wealth of interesting items and features.

Just off the B2026, 3 miles south-east of Edenbridge.

Open daily April to October.

Leeds Castle, Near Maidstone

A large and expansive building that has evolved with a series of alterations and additions from the thirteenth century onwards.

On the B2163 about 4 to 5 miles south-east of Maidstone.

Open daily April to October. November to March Saturday and Sunday only.

Walmer Castle, Near Deal (English Heritage)

Built in the 1550s this is the official residence of the warden of the Cinque Ports, the ancient seaports on the coast of England lying opposite France. The original five (hence the term *cinque*) are Hastings, Sandwich, Dover, Romney and Hythe. Rye and Winchelsea were included later. The Cinque Ports serviced the Royal Navy and in return were granted special privileges and benefits. The office of warden is now mainly ceremonial but the appointment continues to be a much-coveted honour. Sir Winston Churchill held the post for many years.

On the A258 between Deal and Ramsgate around 2 miles south of Deal.

Closed when the lord warden is in residence, but normally open to the public.

LEICESTERSHIRE

Belvoir Castle, Near Grantham

A fire in 1816 destroyed much of the original building, which has since been rebuilt. Particular features of interest are the grand staircase, the furnishings and many famous paintings.

Take the A607 between Melton Mowbray and Grantham. The minor road to the castle is on the north side about 4 miles west of Grantham.

Open daily Easter to September except Monday and Friday and Bank Holidays.

LINCOLNSHIRE

Tattershall Castle, Tattershall (National Trust)

The castle was built around 1440 for Ralph, Lord Cromwell and is built of brick with stone dressings, a most unusual feature for the time. A leisure park adjoins the castle grounds.

On the A153 about 3 to 4 miles south-west of Woodhall Spa.

Open daily except Sunday am.

NORTHAMPTONSHIRE

Rockingham Castle, Near Corby

The original parts of the structure are about 900 years old. Notable features are the massive towers and the gateway. The inside is richly furnished and has a long gallery.

On the A6003 about 2 miles north of Corby.

Open Easter Sunday to September, Sunday, Thursday and Bank Holiday Monday.

NORTHUMBERLAND

Bamburgh Castle, Bamburgh

Set on a crag overlooking the sea, the main features of the remains are the great tower, the gatehouse and part of the curtain wall.

Off the B1340 that connects at both ends with the A1 running between Berwick-upon-Tweed and Alnwick.

Open daily April to October.

Lindisfarne Castle, Holy Island (National Trust)

A sixteenth-century castle restored by Sir Edwin Lutyens. Well furnished with many interesting objects. The castle is approached by a causeway at low tide. Tide tables are displayed at the entrance and can be checked by ringing 01289 330733. Holy Island Kiln and Lindisfarne Priory are nearby (see Appendices B and C)

Open daily April to October except Friday. Phone 01289 389244 for details.

SHROPSHIRE

Stokesay Castle, Near Ludlow (English Heritage)

Built in the thirteenth century, the site is near Shrewsbury School and the Acton Scott Working Farm Museum. A particular feature of the building is the timber-framed gatehouse.

Off the A49 about 8 to 9 miles north-west of Ludlow between Ludlow and Shrewsbury.

Open daily early March to October except Tuesday.

SOMERSET

Nunnery Castle, Near Frome (English Heritage)

The castle was built to an unusual design and has four large circular towers that are still standing.

Off the A361 about 4 miles south-west of Frome between Frome and Wells.

Open daily all year.

STAFFORDSHIRE

Tutbury Castle, Near Burton-on-Trent

Much of the surviving parts date from the fifteenth century, including the north and south towers and the castle wall. The castle was used to imprison Mary Queen of Scots.

On the A50 about 4 to 5 miles west of Burton-on-Trent between Burton and Ashbourne.

Open daily April to October except Thursday. Saturday pm only.

WEST SUSSEX

Arundel Castle, Arundel

The castle has been the home of the Howard family since the Norman Conquest. The dukes have held the position of earl marshal of England since the dukedom of Norfolk was conferred on Sir John Howard by King Richard III in 1483. The castle in its present form is the outcome of a series of additions and alterations. The inside is extravagantly furnished and has impressive collections of paintings and armour.

On the A27 between Chichester and Worthing.

Open daily April to October, closed Sunday.

~

The author considers that the following properties are more suitably described as fortified houses

BERKSHIRE

Donnington Castle, Near Newbury (English Heritage)

A well-fortified house that held out against a siege by Cromwell until much of the building had been badly damaged by cannon fire.

Off the B4494 about 1 mile north of Newbury.

Open daily all year.

KENT

Ightham Mote, Near Sevenoaks (National Trust)

On a minor road between the A21 and the A25, about 6 miles north of Tonbridge and about 4 miles south-east of Sevenoaks.

Open daily April to October excluding Tuesday and Saturday.

LEICESTERSHIRE

Kirby Muxloe Castle, Near Leicester (English Heritage)

The building dates from the fifteenth century and is one of a few from that period to have been built in brick.

Off the B582 about 4 to 5 miles west of Leicester.

Open daily except Wednesday and Thursday. March to October times can vary.

OXFORDSHIRE

Broughton Castle, Near Banbury

An established manor house that dates from 1300. The building was enlarged in Tudor times and featured in the Civil War.

Off the B4033 on the section running between Banbury and Evesham. The building is about 2½ to 3 miles south-west of Banbury.

Open mid-May to September Wednesday and Sunday pm.

~ APPENDIX F ~
HILLFORTS TO VISIT

BUCKINGHAMSHIRE

Ivinghoe Beacon

Just off the B489 between Ivinghoe and Dunstable.

DORSET

Maiden Castle, Near Dorchester (English Heritage)

Off the A354 about 2½ miles south-west of Dorchester.

Open daily all year.

GLOUCESTERSHIRE

Lydney

About 2 miles south-west of Lydney.

HEREFORDSHIRE

Credenhill

On the A480 just north-west of Hereford and south-west of Tillington.

LINCOLNSHIRE

Honington

On the A607 between Grantham and Sleaford.

SUFFOLK

Clare

Some interesting pargeting can also be seen in Clare (see Appendix G).

At the junction between the A1092 and the B1063.

WEST SUSSEX

Cissbury Ring
> From Cissbury Ring there is a pleasant downland walk to Chanctonbury.
> Go into the village of Findon, which is just off the A24, 3 miles north of
> Worthing. Then travel to the village green, where a narrow road leads to
> the ring.

The Trundle
> Close by is the Weald and Downland Open Air Museum which is well worth
> a visit (see Appendix A). Goodwood House is also nearby (see Appendix H
> part B).
> Turn off the A286 at Singleton and take the road to Goodwood. The Trundle
> is next to Goodwood Racecourse.

~ APPENDIX G ~
SELECTED PLACES WITH PARGETING

ESSEX

Coggeshall
> On the A120 between Braintree and Colchester.

Cooksmill Green
> On the A414 between Chelmsford and Chipping Ongar.

Finchingfield
> On the B1053 between Braintree and Haverhill.

Great Waltham
> On the A103 between Chelmsford and Great Dunmow.

Thaxted
> On the B184 between Great Dunmow and Saffron Walden.

HERTFORDSHIRE

Little Hadham
> Just off the A120 between Bishop's Stortford and Standon.

SUFFOLK

Boxford
> Just off the A1071, 15 to 20 miles west of Hadleigh.

Cavendish
  At the junction between the A1092 and the B1064.

Clare
  At the junction between the A1092 and the B1063.

Great Yeldham
  On the the A604 between Sible Hedingham and Haverhill.

Lavenham
  On the A1141 between Hadleigh and Bury St Edmunds.

Stutton
  On the B1080 just south of Ipswich.

Yoxford
  At the junction of the A12 and the A1120 and the B1122 between Saxmundham and Halesworth.

~ APPENDIX H ~
GREAT HOUSES AND GENTRY HOUSES TO VISIT

A: Great Houses

BEDFORDSHIRE

Woburn Abbey, Near Woburn Sands
  The house is part of a Cistercian abbey founded in 1145 and has been in the possession of the dukes of Bedford since the seventeenth century. The building has been continuously restored and improved. The architecture of the west front is Pallandian. Features of note are the cantilevered great staircase, the dining room and the seventeenth-century grotto. A further item of interest is the enfilade, which is a striking example of Baroque architecture. (An enfilade is an arrangement whereby the doorways between a suite of rooms are arranged so that when the doors are open a long vista results, giving a feeling of space).
  Off the A4012 about 10 miles north-west of Dunstable and about 4 miles south-east of Woburn Sands.
  Open daily August to October. January to March, Saturday and Sunday only.

CAMBRIDGESHIRE

Burghley House, Near Stamford

A grand Elizabethan mansion. The Gothic hall has a double hammer-beam roof and a Classical chimney piece. Other interesting parts are the hall staircase, the heaven room, the George room, the vaulted kitchen ceiling and the 'Roman' staircase.

Just off the B1443, which is between Stamford and the Peakirk Wildfowl Refuge. The house is about 1 mile east of Stamford and about 11 miles north-west of Peterborough.

Open daily Easter to early October.

DERBYSHIRE

Chatsworth House, Near Bakewell

The original parts are Elizabethan but much of the present-day structure dates from 1687. Places of particular interest are the blue drawing room, the library, the lower library, the great staircase and the sculpture gallery.

Off the A619 on the section of road between Chesterfield and Bakewell, it can also be reached from the A6 just north of Matlock and from the A621 south of Sheffield.

Open daily August to October.

Haddon Hall, Near Bakewell

One of the finest great houses in Britain. The original parts date from the eleventh century. Much of the building is from the fourteenth century. Notable features are the banqueting hall, the chapel and the long gallery.

Off the A6 approximately 1 to 2 miles south-east of Bakewell.

Open August to October, Tuesday to Sunday and Bank Holiday Mondays. Closed Sunday between July and August, except Bank Holiday Sunday.

Hardwick Hall, Near Mansfield (part National Trust)

A magnificent Elizabethan mansion, which is the creation of Elizabeth, Countess of Shrewsbury, more regularly known as 'Bess of Hardwick'. A particular feature of the house is the size and number of windows. Items of special interest are the high great chamber, the decorated doorways, the long gallery and the main staircase.

Close to the M6 and just off the A617 about 10 miles south-east of Chesterfield and about 7 miles north-west of Mansfield.

Open April to October, Wednesday to Sunday. Bank Holidays pm only.

Kent

Knole, Near Sevenoaks (National Trust)

Most of the main part was built in the mid-fifteenth century by Thomas Bourchier, Archbishop of Canterbury. It was later acquired by Henry VIII. Matters of special interest are the brown gallery, the venetian room, the ambassador's room and the cartoon gallery. The great staircase is a special feature and is believed to be the first time a staircase was designed with the express intent of being the salient feature of the interior.

From the south take the A21 to Sevenoaks and from the north the A225. From the west and east use the A22 (Sevenoaks is close to the M26).

Open April to October, Wednesday to Saturday and Bank Holidays, also Sunday pm.

Penshurst Place, Near Tunbridge Wells

The great hall dates from 1340. The building has been in the ownership of the Sidney family from that date to the present day. Much of the restoration work was undertaken by the late Viscount de Lisle, a former governor general of Australia who won the Victoria Cross in the Second World War. Notable features are the great hall and the long gallery.

Take the turning off the A264 about 4 to 5 miles west of Tunbridge Wells.

Open April to October, Tuesday to Sunday and Bank Holidays.

Norfolk

Holkham Hall, Holkham

A large Palladian-style house built in the mid-eighteenth century on the fringe of the coastal salt marshes. Features of special interest are the long gallery, the marble hall, the enfilade (see also Woburn Abbey), the drawing room, the marble hall gallery and the green state room.

On the A149, 2 miles west of Wells-next-the-Sea.

Open June to September, Sunday, Monday and Thursday. July to August also Wednesday and Bank Holiday Monday.

Houghton Hall, West Rudham

The house was built for Sir Robert Walpole, who was prime minister under George I and George II. Items of particular interest are the stone hall and the great staircase, the marble dining room, the green velvet bedchamber and the drawing room.

Just off the A148 on the section of road between King's Lynn and Fakenham. Houghton Hall is about 1 mile north-west of the village of West Rudham.

Open Easter to September, Wednesday, Thursday, Sunday and Bank Holiday Monday.

NORTH YORKSHIRE

Castle Howard, Near Malton

The house dates from 1699, designed by Sir John Vanbrugh in the English Baroque style. Items of particular interest are the long gallery, the great hall, the surrounding grounds and the dome of the mausoleum.

Take the minor road off the A64 that is about 16 miles north-east of York. Castle Howard is close to Malton, which links the B1257 to the B1248.

Open daily March to October.

Harewood House, Near Leeds

Built in the mid-1700s, though changes and additions have taken place in more modern times. The house is beautifully furnished and features of special note are the long gallery, the library and the cinnamon drawing room.

Just off the A61 between Leeds and Wakefield. The turning is 6 to 7 miles north of Leeds.

Open daily April to October. February, March and November, Sunday only.

OXFORDSHIRE

Blenheim Palace, Woodstock

The palace was built for the first Duke of Marlborough as a reward for his victory at the battle of Blenheim in 1704. The architect was Sir John Vanbrugh. Sir Winston Churchill was born at the palace, where he spent much of his childhood.

Take the turning off the A34 at Woodstock.

Open daily mid-March to October.

WILTSHIRE

Longleat, Near Frome

Splendid Elizabethan house built of Bath stone with extensive grounds landscaped by Capability Brown. The house is the seat of the Marquis of Bath. Features of note are the great hall and the ornate and delicately carved chimney piece in the great hall, as well as the Renaissance-style roofline, the red library and the Bishop Ken library.

Off the A350 on the section of road between Shaftesbury and Warminster and about 4 to 5 miles south of Frome just off the A362.

House open daily. Park open daily mid-March to October.

Wilton House, Near Wilton

The present building dates from the 1340s but many alterations and additions were made in the seventeenth century with the involvement of Inigo Jones. The property is the seat of the Earl of Pembroke. Matters of special note are the drawing room/ballroom, known as the double blue room (so

called because the length, which is 60 feet, is exactly double the width of
30 feet). Also the Gothic vaulted cloistered corridor, the private drawing
room and the single cube bedroom. The south front is worth an inspection,
and although generally regarded as Renaissance, lacks the influence of the
Classical orders.

Off the A30 between Wilton and Salisbury.

Open daily Easter to October except Monday and Bank Holiday Monday.

West Sussex

Petworth House, Near Midhurst (National Trust)

Some parts date from the early fourteenth century but most of the structure was
built in the late 1600s. The magnificent parkland was created by Capability
Brown. Items of note are the north gallery, the carved room, the white library,
the grand staircase, the picture gallery and the spacious ice house.

On the A272 between Midhurst and Billingshurst. The house is about 6 to 7
miles east of Midhurst.

Open August to October, afternoons Tuesday, Thursday, Saturday, Sunday
and Bank Holiday Monday.

B: Gentry Houses

Avon

Clevedon Court, Near Clevedon (National Trust)

The mansion was built in 1320 and has altered little from that time. Exhibited
in the house is an exquisite collection of fine glassware. About a mile from
the house is a craft centre, where a number of ancient crafts are still carried
out.

Just off the B3130, about ½ to ¾ of a mile east of Clevedon, which is close to
the M5.

Open April to October, Wednesday, Thursday, Sunday and Bank Holiday
Monday pm.

Berkshire

Basildon Park, Near Pangbourne (National Trust)

Built in the 1700s from Bath stone, the house is in the Classical style. It was
restored in the latter part of the last century and refurnished with fine
furniture, fittings and paintings. An unusual feature is the octagonal
drawing room.

Off the A329 heading towards Oxford, about 1½ to 2 miles north of
Pangbourne.

Open April to October, Wednesday to Sunday pm and Bank Holiday Monday.

Swallowfield, Near Swallowfield Village

> The house was built in 1690 and remodelled in the eighteenth century. A notable feature is the oval vestibule. The elegant doorway at the entrance to the walled garden was designed by William Talman.
>
> Off the B3349 about 5 to 6 miles south-east of Reading.
>
> Open May to September, Wednesday and Thursday pm.

BUCKINGHAMSHIRE

Chicheley Hall, Near Newport Pagnell

> Built between 1719 and 1793, the house is in the English Baroque style. The internal fittings are to an exceptionally high standard. The hinged panels in the library, which protect the books, are probably unique. The present owners are descendants of Admiral Beatty and they exhibit a collection of naval memorabilia.
>
> Just off the A422 around 2 to 3 miles north-east of Newport Pagnell.
>
> Open daily Easter to September and Bank Holiday Monday pm.

Dorney Court, Near Eton

> The house was built around 1440 and has heavily ornamented brickwork. Notable features include the great chamber, the hall and the beamed parlour.
>
> Off the B3026 about 2 to 2½ miles west of Eton.
>
> Open Easter weekend, then Easter to October, Sunday and Bank Holiday Monday. June to September, Monday and Tuesday pm.

CAMBRIDGESHIRE

Burghley House, Near Stamford

> A grand Elizabethan mansion with spires and ornamental chimneys. There are 18 state rooms extravagantly furnished. The heaven room is profusely decorated with mythological scenes.
>
> Take the A15 north of Peterborough and then the B1443. The house is about 2 miles east of Stamford and some 10 to 12 miles north-west of Peterborough.
>
> Open daily Easter to early October.

CHESHIRE

Aldington Hall, Near Bollington

> Parts of the house date from 1581 and there is a superb hammer-beam roof and fine murals. The exterior is in the finest tradition of the black-and-white timber buildings of the area. The red-brick addition dates from 1757.
>
> Just off the A523 about 5 to 6 miles north of Macclesfield, and just south of the boundary of Greater Manchester.
>
> Open Good Friday to September, Sunday and Bank Holiday. August, also Wednesday and Saturday pm.

Little Moreton Hall, Near Congleton (National Trust)
> A wonderful jettied timber building with intricate panelling – a heritage gem. Notable features are the long gallery, the drawing room and the tapestries, as well as the furniture, which includes work by Thomas Chippendale.
> Just off the A34 between Congleton and Kidsgrove – each about 4 to 5 miles distance.
> Hall open daily pm June to September, excluding Monday. April to May, Tuesday, Thursday, Saturday and Sunday pm. October, Sunday and Saturday pm only.

Tatton Park, Near Knutsford (National Trust)
> The house was built in the late eighteenth century by Samuel Wyatt. The grounds were designed by Humphry Repton. Notable features are the great drawing room, the music room and the columned entrance hall.
> Off the A50 3 to 4 miles north of Knutsford (Knutsford is close to the M6).
> Park and gardens open daily all year round. Selective times for viewing the house – make enquires through local tourist office.

CORNWALL

Cotehele House, Near Calstock (National Trust)
> A large granite house built in the late fifteenth century. The medieval atmosphere and furnishings have been carefully preserved, which give a particular feel to life in earlier times. There is also a medieval dovecote and a restored watermill.
> Take the A390 between Tavistock and Callington and cross the river at Albaston and turn south, then follow the minor roads to Cothele House. Alternatively take a minor road to Calstock from the A390 and at Calstock take a minor road to Cotehele House.
> Open daily March to November, except Friday.

Godolphin House, Near Helston
> A substantial Tudor mansion with battlemented parapets and a double-sided front entrance loggia that was added in the 1630s.
> Off the B3302 about 7 to 8 miles north-west of Helston.
> Open May to June, Thursday pm. July to September, Tuesday and Thursday.

Lanhydrock, Near Bodmin (National Trust)
> The original part of the house dates from the seventeenth century but a large proportion was restored in 1881 after extensive fire damage. The front elevation is plain and battlemented. Notable features are the north wing gallery, the main bedrooms and the kitchen.
> On the B3268 about 2 miles south of Bodmin.
> Open daily August to October. November to March gardens only.

St Michael's Mount, Near Penzance (National Trust)

The site has an interesting history with the present house having been a priory. Special features are the blue dining room and the lady chapel. A beacon on the chapel tower gave warning of the Spanish Armada. There are some exceptional views to be seen from the site.

Located at Marazion near Penzance close to the A394.

Open April to May, Monday, Tuesday, Wednesday, Friday. June to October, Monday to Friday. November to March, Monday, Wednesday, Thursday, Friday.

CUMBRIA

Levens Hall, Near Kendal

The hall dates from 1250 and is noted for the elaborate interior, especially the plasterwork and the carved panelling. In the original brew house there is an interesting collection of old steam engines.

On the A6 about 5 miles south of Kendal.

Open Easter Sun to early October, Sunday to Thursday.

DERBYSHIRE

Kedleston Hall, Near Derby (National Trust)

Designed by Robert Adam in 1759, the building is a fine example of the neo-Classical style. Items of note are the grand portico, the marble entrance hall, the library, the state rooms and the domed saloon.

Off the A52 about 4 to 4½ miles north-west of Derby. The minor road to Kedleston Hall also connects to the A6.

Open August to September, Saturday, Sunday and Monday pm.

Sudbury Hall, Near Uttoxeter (National Trust)

A feature of the exterior is intricately worked stone, contrasting with the pale and deep red patterned brickwork. The interior is rich in decorative arts.

Off the A50 on the section of road between Uttoxeter and Derby. The house is some 5 to 6 miles east of Uttoxeter.

Open April to October, Wednesday to Sunday and Bank Holiday Monday.

DEVON

Buckland Abbey, Near Yelverton (National Trust)

Formerly the home of Sir Francis Drake, the house contains many relics from his exploits. In the hall is the famous Drake's drum and some interesting documents relating to the Armada are on view.

Off the A386 about 12 miles north of Plymouth.

Open daily July to October. November to March, Wednesday, Saturday and Sunday.

Powderham Castle, Near Exmouth

    The building dates from 1390 but was converted from a castle to a mansion in the eighteenth century. The principal rooms have finely worked plaster and marble fireplaces. A feature of special interest is the staircase and hall.

    Off the A379 about 10 miles south-east of Exeter and around 3 miles from Exmouth.

    Open for viewing mid-May to September, Sunday to Thursday pm.

HAMPSHIRE

Stratfield Saye House, Swallowfield

    A substantial seventeenth-century mansion which was presented to the Duke of Wellington in recognition of his victory over Napoleon at Waterloo. The hall is full of items and paintings connected with his military achievements. The library is almost unchanged since the time of the 'Iron Duke'.

    The house is on the section of the A33 running between Basingstoke and Reading. It is about 5 to 6 miles north-east of Basingstoke.

    Open daily May to September except Friday. Also Easter and weekends in April.

The Vine, Near Basingstoke (National Trust)

    The main body of the house has been built in attractive pink and dark-red brick. The north elevation is in the Classical style and has a large portico. The interior decorations and furnishings are to a high standard and include a prominent staircase, fluted columns and intricate plasterwork.

    Off the A340 about 4 miles north of Basingstoke.

    Open daily April to mid-October pm, excluding Monday and Friday. Also Bank Holiday Monday.

HEREFORDSHIRE

Hanbury Hall, Near Droitwich (National Trust)

    A fine Queen Anne house in red brick that has been furnished with taste and care. Very few changes have been made since the house was built. The long room contains an exceptionally fine collection of English porcelain.

    Off the B4090 about 3 miles east of Droitwich.

    Open April to October, Saturday, Sunday and, Bank Holiday Monday pm. May to September, Wednesday and Sunday pm.

HERTFORDSHIRE

Knebworth House, Knebworth

> The house is of Tudor origin but has undergone extensive alterations in the
> the Victorian Gothic style. Internally some of the Tudor elements remain,
> including the banqueting hall and the Queen Elizabeth room.
>
> On the A1(M) about 1 mile south of Stevenage.
>
> Open daily mid-May to September except Monday. April to May, weekends
> and Bank Holidays.

HUMBERSIDE

Burton Constable, Near Hull

> A fine Tudor residence in red brick with castellated towers and stone-
> mullioned oriel windows. Rooms of particular interest are the hall, the long
> gallery and the dining room.
>
> Off the B1238 about 12 miles north-east of Hull.
>
> Open daily Easter to September pm, excluding Friday and Saturday.

KENT

Chartwell, Near Westerham (National Trust)

> Compared to others on the list this house is modest, plain and unpretentious
> but it was the home of Sir Winston Churchill for many years. The rooms
> have a number of interesting aspects of his life.
>
> Open April to October, Tuesday, Wednesday and Thursday pm. Otherwise
> viewing times are varied.

LANCASHIRE

Rufford Old Hall, Near Eccleston (National Trust)

> An early sixteenth-century timber-framed house with an open hall. The
> elevations are in fine black-and-white timber panelling and are a superb
> legacy of the period. Items of special note are the spere posts and screen.
> On exhibition is a collection of sixteenth-century weaponry and armour.
>
> Off the A59 on the section between Ormskirk and Preston. The hall is about 6
> miles north-east of Ormskirk.
>
> Open daily April to October, except Friday.

LINCOLNSHIRE

Doddington Hall, Near Lincoln

> Built in the seventeenth century, the house is a mixture of brick and stone
> with large mullioned windows. The roof has three large cupolas. Internally
> there is some exceptionally fine plasterwork.
>
> On the B1190 4 to 5 miles west of Lincoln.
>
> Open daily May to September, Sunday and Bank Holidays pm only.

NORFOLK
Blickling Hall, Near Aylsham (National Trust)
  The house is fourteenth century but has undergone extensive alterations.
    Noted features are the Peter the Great room, the long gallery and the
    staircase.
  Located just off the B1354, the house is 1 to 2 miles north-west of Aylsham.
  Open daily April to October pm excluding Monday and Thursday. Also open
    Bank Holiday Monday.

NORTHAMPTONSHIRE
Althorp, Near Northampton
  Althorp has been the home of the Spencer family since 1508 and was the
    childhood home of Diana, Princess of Wales. Notable features are the long
    gallery, the Georgian rooms and the portico. There is also an exhibition of
    rare porcelain.
  On the A428 on the section of road between Northampton and Rugby. The
    house is about 5 to 6 miles north-west of Northampton.
  Open daily, except just am from October to June.

NORTHUMBERLAND
Prudhoe Castle, Prudhoe (English Heritage)
  Behind the gatehouse of the original medieval castle is a grand nineteenth-
    century manor house. The site has been in the ownership of the Percy
    family since 1351. The house is furnished and decorated in the Georgian
    style.
  Off the A695 about 5 miles west of Newcastle-Upon-Tyne.
  Open daily April to September. October to March daily except Wednesday
    and every alternate Friday.

Wallington House, Near Morpeth (National Trust)
  Built in 1688, the mansion underwent substantial changes during the
    eighteenth century. Notable features include the central hall, the library,
    the dining room and the saloon.
  On the B6343 about 15 to 16 miles west of Morpeth, and a similar distance
    from Newcastle-upon-Tyne when using the A696, which connects to the
    B6342.
  Open daily April to September, except Tuesday.

NORTH YORKSHIRE

Nunnington Hall, Nunnington (National Trust)

Part of the building dates from the sixteenth century but a number of alterations and additions have been made in later times. Many of the rooms have been tastefully decorated in the seventeenth-century style. Much of the joinery, including the panelling is noteworthy.

Take the section of the B1257 running between Malton and Helmsley. The house is about 4 to 5 miles south-east of Helsmsley.

Open May to October, Tuesday, Thursday, Saturday, Sunday and Bank Holiday Monday pm.

OXFORDSHIRE

Mapledurham House, Near Caversham

A red-brick Elizabethan mansion. Notable features are the staircase and the carvings in the entrance to the hall. The house was the home of the Blount family who were noted Roman Catholics. A small window at the top of the house is studded with oyster shells – this was used as a sign of safe refuge for Catholics during times of persecution. Near to the house is a watermill which is still in operation.

Off the A4074 around 4 to 5 miles north-west of Reading (Reading is close to the M4).

House, water mill and park are open from Easter Sunday to late September, Saturday, Sunday and Bank Holiday pm.

Stonor Park, Stonor

The house dates from the twelfth century and has been in the ownership of the Stonor family for 800 years. As staunch Roman Catholics the family provided refuge and cover to Catholics suffering persecution during periods of religious conflict. In the roof is a secret room once used by Edward Campion, who was later tried, tortured and executed for his belief.

Off the B480 about 2 miles north of Stonor and about 5 miles from Henley-on-Thames.

Open April, Sunday pm and Easter Mondy. May to September, Wednesday, Thursday and Sunday pm, and Bank Holiday Monday. Also Saturday pm during August.

SHROPSHIRE

Benthall Hall, Near Much Wenlock (National Trust)

A stone-built Elizabethan mansion with mullioned windows and tall brick chimneys. Notable features are the intricately carved staircase, the oak panelling and the fine seventeenth-century plasterwork. The house was the home of the Benthall family who were strict Roman Catholics during the time of persecution. They had a secret priest's hole built within the house.

Off the B4375 about 4 to 5 miles north-east of Much Wenlock.

Open April to September, Tuesday, Wednesday, Sunday and Bank Holiday Monday pm.

SOUTH YORKSHIRE

Bramham Park, Near Tadcaster

A fine Queen Anne mansion with two wings linked by colonnades. The interior has fine furnishings, porcelain, silver and paintings.

Off the A1 on the section of road running between Garforth and Wetherby. The house is about 5 miles south of Wetherby.

Open mid-June to August, Sunday, Tuesday, Wednesday, Thursday and Bank Holiday pm.

SUFFOLK

Ickworth, Near Bury St Edmunds (National Trust)

A large eighteenth-century manor house with a spectacular rotunda containing the drawing room, dining room, library and entrance hall. The rooms are extravagantly furnished and there are fine collections of silver, porcelain and paintings.

Take the A143 south from Bury St Edmunds towards Haverhill. The house is about 3 miles south of Bury St Edmunds.

Open daily pm May to September, excluding Monday and Thursday. October to April, weekends and Bank Holidays pm.

SURREY

Clandon Park, Near Guildford (National Trust)

The house was built by a Venetian architect in 1733. The south elevation is mainly Georgian but there are many Venetian features elsewhere. Notable features are the marble hall, the chimney pieces and the plaster ceilings.

On the A247 about 3 miles east of Guildford.

Open daily April to October, excluding Thursday and Friday.

Loseley House, Near Guildford
> A fine stone-built Elizabethan mansion with mullioned windows. The house
> was host to Elizabeth I on three occasions and James I was a frequent
> visitor.
> On the B3000 about 2 miles south of Guildford.
> Open May to September, Wednesday to Saturday, also spring and summer
> Bank Holidays.

WARWICKSHIRE

Ragley Hall, Near Alcester
> The house was designed by Robert Hook in 1680 and is in the Palladian style.
> The quality of the work inside is exceptional, especially the south staircase
> and the fine murals. The great hall is also spectacular and is the work of
> James Gibbs.
> On the A435 about 2 miles south of Alcester.
> Open daily April to October except Monday and Friday.

WEST SUSSEX

Goodwood House, Goodwood
> A seat of the third Duke of Richmond, the house was built in the eighteenth
> century and designed by James Wyatt. An unusual feature is the fact that it
> has been built of local flint – a practice seldom used in the grand houses of
> the time. The house is richly furnished and has played host to most of the
> kings and queens of Europe during Goodwood Race week. The trundle
> hillfort is nearby and the Weald and Downland Open-Air Museum is about
> 2 miles further towards Midhurst. (The museum is a fascinating day out
> and well worth a visit.)
> Take the A286 between Chichester and Midhurst and then the minor road
> to Goodwood. Alternatively the A285 running between Chichester and
> Petworth and then a minor road to Goodwood.
> Open Easter weekend, and Sunday and Monday afternoons from early March
> to early October. Also Tuesday, Wednesday and Thursday pm in August.
> Advise checking by phone before viewing – 01243 774107.

Parham House, Near Pulborough
> An exceptionally fine Elizabethan mansion. A special feature is the great hall
> where Elizabeth I dined in state in 1593. The house is full of interesting
> items of furniture and paintings. Other features of note are the great
> parlour, the saloon, the great chamber, the green room and the gallery.
> Off the A283 on the section of road between Storrington and Pulborough. The
> house is about 3 miles south of Pulborough.
> Open from Easter Sunday to early October, Sunday, Wednesday and Thursday
> afternoons, and Bank Holiday Monday.

Uppark, Near South Harting (National Trust)

The house was built around 1690 and underwent extensive alterations and additions in 1750. The entrance portico was not built until 1811. In 1989 the property was badly damaged by fire and has since been completely restored. Places of particular interest are the dining room, the stone hall, the saloon, the tapestry bedroom and the little dining room.

On the B2146, 5 to 6 miles south-east of Petersfield. The house is about 1 mile south of South Harting.

Open April to September, Wednesday, Thursday, Sunday and Bank Holiday Monday afternoons.

Stansted House, Near Funtington

The original part of the house was built in 1688 but has since undergone much rebuilding, especially after a devastating fire in 1900. Places of interest are the main hall, the stairway, the library, the main drawing room and the blue drawing room. The chapel nearby is unique as it is the only Christian Church where a window (the east window) is wholly Jewish in symbolism.

Take the B2147 running between Westbourne (Near Havant) and Funtington. At Funtington take the minor road to Rowland's Castle and follow the signs.

Open Easter Sunday to September, Sunday and Monday pm. July to August, Sunday to Wednesday. See www.stansteadpark.co.uk for programme of functions and activities.

WILTSHIRE

Littlecote, Near Hungerford

The house dates from 1415 and was once the home of Sir John Popham, the Lord Chief Justice who presided at the trials of Sir Walter Raleigh and Guy Fawkes. The house is full of interest with paintings and various displays.

Off the B4192 on the section of road running between Hungerford and Swindon. The house is about 2 to 3 miles north-west of Hungerford.

Open daily April to October.

～ APPENDIX I ～
MILLS TO VISIT

AVON

Priston Mill, Near Bath

A water-powered corn mill which produces stoneground wholemeal flour.

Off the B3115 which runs between the A39 and the A367. The mill is 4 to 5 miles south-east of Bath.

Open Easter to September (check times of opening).

BEDFORDSHIRE

Bromham Mill, Near Bedford

A water mill that has been turned into a milling museum.

Just off the A428 about 3 miles west of Bedford.

Open August to October, Thursday, Saturday, Sunday and Bank Holiday Monday pm.

Stevington Mill, Near Bedford

A post mill (windmill) built around 1770 which has been recently restored.

On a minor road between the A428 and the A6. The mill is about 6 miles west of Bedford.

The mill can be viewed by contacting the Royal George Inn, Stevington, for access: 01234 228330.

CAMBRIDGESHIRE

Houghton Mill, Near St Ives (National Trust)

A brick- and timber-boarded water mill, most of which dates from the seventeenth century.

Off the A1123 between Huntingdon and St Ives. The mill is about 2 miles east of Huntingdon.

Open mid-April to mid-September pm, except Thursday and Friday. Mid-September to mid-October, Saturday and Sunday pm.

Sacrewell Mill, Near Peterborough

A working watermill which is also used to display past farming skills and methods.

Off the A47 close to where it joins the A1. The mill is about 6 to 7 miles west of Peterborough.

Open April to October, Sunday and Bank Holidays.

CHESHIRE

Quarry Bank Mill, Near Wilmslow (National Trust)

A water-powered industrial mill built in 1784.

Near the B5166 on the section of road running between Wilmslow and Manchester. The mill is about 2 miles north of Wilmslow.

Open daily June to September. October to May, Tuesday to Sunday and Bank Holiday Monday.

Stretton Mill, Near Wrexham

A corn-grinding watermill which has been restored as a working museum.

On a minor road off the A534 close to where it joins the A41. The mill is about 10 miles south of Chester.

Open April to October, Tuesday to Sunday, and Bank Holiday Monday.

CUMBRIA

Eskdale Mill, Eskdale

Approached by a seventeenth-century packhorse bridge, the mill dates from Elizabethan times. Recently restored, it houses an exhibition on old milling techniques and traditions.

On a minor road leading off the A595 about 4 miles south of Gosforth and 5 to 6 miles north-east of Ravenglass.

Open daily Easter to September except Saturday.

Heron Mill, Near Storth

A long history of milling is associated with the site. The present mill was built in 1750 and following recent restoration is in full working order.

Off the A6 about 1 mile south of Milnthorpe.

Open daily April to September except Monday and Bank Holidays.

Wythop Mill, Near Cockermouth

A water-powered mill built some time during the eighteenth century. It was later converted from grinding corn to sawing wood. It now houses a woodworking museum.

Off the A66 on the section between Cockermouth and Keswick. The mill is about 5 miles east of Cockermouth.

Open daily March to October except Monday. October to February, Saturday and Sunday.

DERBYSHIRE

Cromford Mill, Near Matlock

A water-driven cotton mill built in 1771 by Richard Arkwright.

Off the A6 about 3 miles south of Matlock (also close to the Peak District Mining Museum).

Open daily February to October except Monday. November to January, Sunday.

DEVON

Bickleigh Mill, Near Tiverton

A restored watermill which is now being used to make and retail rural craft products.

On the A396 south of Tiverton.

Open daily Easter to Christmas. New Year to Easter, Saturday and Sunday.

ESSEX

Bourne Mill, Near Colchester (National Trust)

Built in 1591, it was first used for grinding corn, later converted for cloth making before then being reused for grinding corn.

Off the B1025 about 1 mile south of Colchester.

Open April to mid-October, Saturday, Sunday and Bank Holiday Monday pm. Also July to September, Tuesday pm.

LINCOLNSHIRE

Alvingham Mill, Near Louth

A water-driven mill built in the late seventeenth century which is now a working museum.

On a minor road off the A16 between Louth and Cleethorpes. The mill is 2½ to 3 miles north-east of Louth.

Open July to August, Monday to Thursday, and then every second and fourth Sunday pm.

Burgh Le March Mill, Near Skegness

A wind-driven mill built about 1813, used for grinding corn.

On the A158 about 4 to 5 miles west of Skegness.

Open daily. When the wind is suitable the mill is in operation on the second and last Sunday of each month and on Bank Holiday weekends.

Heckington Mill, Near Sleaford
>   Built in 1830 the mill is the only eight-sailed windmill surviving in Britain. Since restoration it has been used to house rural craft workshops.
>   On the B1394 which connects to the A52 and the A17. The mill is about 5 to 6 miles east of Sleaford.
>   Open April to September, Saturday, Sunday and Bank Holidays pm.

Sibsey Mill, Near Boston (English Heritage)
>   A large brick-built tower windmill which is one of the few surviving six-sailed mills left in England. The mill houses a display on the Lincolnshire milling industry.
>   Off the B1184 close to where it joins the A16 running between Boston and Spilsby. The mill is around 4 to 5 miles north of Boston.
>   Open April to September, Thursday, Friday and Saturday. Also Wednesday am and Sunday pm.

NORFOLK

Cley Mill, Cley-next-to-the-Sea
>   A wind-driven mill built in the early eighteenth century and now used as a nature look-out and bird sanctuary by the Norfolk Naturalists' Trust.
>   Cley is on the coast road between Sheringham and Wells-next-to-the Sea.
>   Open daily early-May to September pm.

NORTHUMBERLAND

Heatherslaw Mill, Near Coldstream
>   A twin watermill, one of which is still in working order. Visitors can watch grain being ground and barley hulled and polished.
>   Off the B6354 close to the junction with the B6353 and the B6352.
>   Open daily April to September. October, Saturday and Sunday.

Otterburn Mill, Otterburn
>   A watermill has stood on the site since 1245. The existing mill is still being used for spinning and weaving tweeds. The products being made on site can be purchased from a shop nearby.
>   Off the A696 close to where it joins the A68.
>   Open May to December, Monday to Saturday. January to April, Monday to Friday.

NOTTINGHAMSHIRE

Green's Mill, Near Nottingham

A fine five-storey and four-sailed tower mill which is still operational. The mill was once owned by George Green, a noted Cambridge University mathematician. Adjoining the mill is a scientific exhibition detailing the contribution George Green made to science.

Off the A612 about 2½ miles east of Nottingham town centre.

Open daily except Monday and Tuesday, including Bank Holidays.

North Leverton Mill, Near East Retford

A working windmill still in commercial operation.

From East Retford take the A620 going east. On leaving the town take the minor road to North Leverton. The mill is about 4 miles from East Retford.

Open during working hours.

SOMERSET

Perry's Cider Mill, Near Ilminster

A water-driven mill still used to press apples in the cider-making process.

Off the A303 about 1½ to 2 miles south of Ilminster.

Open daily during working hours.

STAFFORDSHIRE

Brindley Mill, Near Leek

A water-driven corn mill built in 1752.

On the A523 about 1 mile north-west of Leek.

Open Easter to October, Saturday, Sunday and Bank Holiday Monday. Also Monday, Tuesday and Thursday pm in July and August.

SUFFOLK

Pakenham Mills, Near Bury St Edmunds

There are two mills to view. A well-preserved tower windmill and a water-driven mill. Both are still being used to grind corn in the traditional manner.

Take the minor road running between the A143 and the A1088. The mills are about 5 to 6 miles north-east of Bury St Edmunds.

Open Easter and May to September, Wednesday, Saturday, Sunday and Bank Holidays.

Saxstead Green Post Mill, Near Framlingham (English Heritage)
 The mill dates from 1796 and is a fine example of a post mill.
 Take the A1120 running between Stowmarket and the junction with the A12.
   The mill is on the north side of the A1120 about 2 to 3 miles north-west of
   Framlingham.
 Open daily April to September, except Sunday.

Woodbridge Tide Mill, Woodbridge
 The mill dates from the eighteenth century and is one of a limited number
   of tide mills built in England. The mill operates 2 hours either side of the
   tide. The building was restored in 1968.
 Located on the estuary just south of Woodbridge.
 Open daily July to September.

SURREY

Outwood Mill, Near Smallfield
 The mill is the oldest working post mill (windmill) in England.
 On a minor road off the A23 on the section runing between Horley and
   Reigate. The mill is about 5 miles south-east of Reigate. Reigate is close to
   the M25 and the M23.
 Open Easter to October, Sunday and Bank Holiday Monday pm.

WEST SUSSEX

Woods Mill, Near Henfield
 An eighteenth-century watermill which has a display featuring the history of
   the mill.
 Off the A2037 on the section of road running between Henfield and the
   junction with the A283 near Steyning. The mill is about 1 mile south of
   Henfield.
 Open Good Friday to September, Tuesday, Wednesday, Thursday and
   Saturday pm. Also Bank Holidays.

~ Appendix J ~
Pottery Kilns to Visit

Cornwall

Wheal Martyn China Clay Heritage Site, Carthew

An interesting display in the methods used in the winning and working of clay and kaolin used in the manufacture of porcelain.

Take the A391 from St Austell to Bodmin and then the minor road signposted to Carthew which is about 1 to 1½ miles from St Austell.

Open daily May to September. October to April, closed Saturday to Wednesday.

Herefordshire and Worcestershire

Museum of Worcester Porcelain, Worcester.

The factory was built in 1749. The museum has interesting displays of porcelain development and manufacture.

Open daily.

Staffordshire

Gladstone Pottery Museum, Near Stoke-on-Trent

On view are a number of bottle kilns. All aspects of pottery production can be seen in the museum.

Off the A50 about 3 miles south-east of Stoke-on-Trent.

Open daily April to October except Monday.

Wedgwood Visitor Centre, Barlaston

The famous Wedgwood pottery first went into production in 1775. The centre gives a fascinating insight into the production and development of china.

Take the A51 running between Stoke-on-Trent and Stone and then the minor road signposted to Barlaston. Barlaston is about 2½ to 3 miles south of Stoke.

Open daily.

~ APPENDIX K ~
BLAST FURNACES TO VISIT

DURHAM

Derwentcote Steel Furnace, Hamsterley (English Heritage)
One of the oldest surviving blast furnaces in England. Built in the early
eighteenth century.
Off the 694 between Hamsterley and Rowland's Gill.
Open daily March to September. October to February, first and third Sundays.

SHROPSHIRE

Ironbridge Gorge Museum, Telford
Houses the original Abraham Darby furnace of 1709, which was rebuilt in
1777.
South-west of Telford near the village of Broseley.
Open daily March to October. Helpful information available at the visitor
centre.

YORKSHIRE

Abbeydale Complex, Sheffield
This is a working complex showing furnacing to processing and the making of
various artefacts from iron.
Open April to October, Monday to Thursday, and Sunday.

~ APPENDIX L ~
GUNPOWDER MUSEUMS TO VISIT

ESSEX

Royal Gunpowder Mills, Waltham Abbey
Waltham Abbey is between Cheshunt and Epping. From the M25 junction 26
take the A121 to Waltham Abbey, or from junction 25 go to Waltham Cross
and then take the A121.
Ring to check opening times.

Kent

Chart Gunpowder Mills, Faversham
> Faversham is close to the M2 between Sittingbourne and Canterbury. From the M2 take the Faversham turning then left on to the A2, then get on to the B2040 and follow the signs to the mills.
> Open Easter to end of October, Saturday, Sunday and Bank holidays pm.

~ Appendix M ~
Museums that Feature
Historical Brickwork

West Sussex

Amberley Museum, Near Arundel
> Off the B2139 about 5 miles north of Arundel. The museum is close to Amberley railway station.
> Open April to October, Wednesday to Sunday and Bank Holidays.

Weald and Downland Open-Air Museum, Singleton, Near Chichester
> The site is close to Goodwood Racecourse and the Trundle.
> Open daily April to October. November to March, Wednesday, Sunday and most Bank Holidays.

Worcestershire

Avoncroft Museum of Buildings, Near Bromsgrove
> The site is off the A38 about 2 miles from Bromsgrove.
> Open daily June to August. Restricted opening thereafter.

Tourist Information Offices

MAIN OFFICE

English Tourist Board
1 Palace Street
London
SW1E 5HE
Tel: 0207 578 1400
Website: www.enjoyengland.com

REGIONAL OFFICES

Brighton and Hove Visitor Information Centre
10 Bartholomew Square
Brighton
BN1 1JS
Tel: 0300 300 0088
Website: www.visitbrighton.com

Leamington Spa Tourist Information Centre
The Royal Pump Rooms
Royal Leamington Spa
CV32 4AB
Tel: 01926 742762
Website: www.shakespeare-country.co.uk

Manchester Tourist Information Centre
Town Hall Extension
St Peter's Square
Manchester
M60 2LA
Tel: 0161 234 3157
Website: www.visitmanchester.com

Northumbria Tourist Board
Aykley Heads
Durham
DH1 5UX
Tel: 0191 375 3000
Website: www.visitnorthumbria.com

Portsmouth Visitor Information Service
Clarence Esplanade
Southsea
Hampshire
PO5 3PB
Tel: 02392 826722
Website: www.visitportsmouth.co.uk

Somerset Tourism
County Hall
Taunton
TA1 4DY
Tel: 01823 355255.
Website: www.celebratingsomerset.com

South East England Tourist Board
The Old Brew House
Warwick Park
Tunbridge Wells
Kent
TN2 5TU
Tel: 01892 540766.
Website: www.southeastengland.com

Southport Tourist Information Centre
112 Lord Street
Southport
PR8 1NY
Tel: 01704 533333
Website: www.visit-southport.org.uk

Stratford Tourist Information Centre
Bridgefoot
Stratford-upon-Avon
CV37 6GW
Tel: 01789 293127
Website: www.shakespeare-country.co.uk

Warwick Tourist Information Centre
Court House
Jury Street
Warwick
CV34 4EW
Tel: 01926 492212.
Website: www.warwick-uk.co.uk

Yorkshire Tourist Board
312 Tadcaster Road
York
YO24 1GS
Tel: 01904 707961
Website: www.yorkshirevisitor.com

Index